PENGUIN
COMPASS

COMPASS

HOW TO FIND THE WORK YOU LOVE

Laurence G. Boldt is a writer and career consultant based in the San Francisco Bay area. He is the author of *Zen and the Art of Making a Living* and *Zen Soup*.

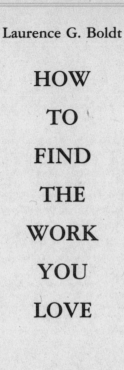

Laurence G. Boldt

HOW
TO
FIND
THE
WORK
YOU
LOVE

PENGUIN COMPASS

COMPASS

Published by the Penguin Group
Penguin Putnam Inc., 375 Hudson Street, New York, New York 10014, U.S.A.
Penguin Books Ltd, 27 Wrights Lane, London W8 5TZ, England
Penguin Books Australia Ltd, Ringwood, Victoria, Australia
Penguin Books Canada Ltd, 10 Alcorn Avenue, Toronto, Ontario, Canada M4V 3B2
Penguin Books (N.Z.) Ltd, 182–190 Wairau Road, Auckland 10, New Zealand

Penguin Books Ltd, Registered Offices: Harmondsworth, Middlesex, England

First published in Arkana 1996

11 13 15 17 19 20 18 16 14 12 10

Grateful acknowledgment is made for permission to reprint an excerpt from *The Family Reunion: A Play* by T. S. Eliot. Copyright 1939 by T. S. Eliot and renewed 1967 by Esme Valerie Eliot. Reprinted by permission of Harcourt Brace & Company and Faber and Faber Ltd.

LIBRARY OF CONGRESS CATALOGING IN PUBLICATION DATA
Boldt, Laurence G.
How to find the work you love/Laurence G. Boldt
p.   cm.
ISBN 0 14 01.9524 6
1. Vocational interests.   2. Vocational guidance.   I. Title.
HF5381.5.B65 1996
650.14—dc20   95–33476

Printed in the United States of America
Set in Garamond No. 3
Designed by Fritz Metsch

To that unnamable something which calls us all to be what we truly are.

Acknowledgments

Much of the material in this book was first developed for *How to Find the Work You Love* seminars, which I began conducting across the country in the early 1990s. I would like to thank all those who attended for your feedback and enthusiastic response. It was a great joy and privilege to share in the energy and excitement which you generated at these events.

In addition, special thanks are due several people who helped to make this book possible. Thanks to Kim Grant for her editorial assistance and tenacious commitment to excellence, and for being there so many times when it really counted. Thanks to Tina Kolaas for her help in editing and for her inspirational support, especially in the early stages of the project. Finally, many thanks to Susan Shapiro for assisting with the design and layout of the self-published edition.

Contents

Introduction

The Changing Nature of Work

The trouble with the rat race is that even if you win, you're still a rat.

—LILY TOMLIN

THE RAT RACE. The fast track. The old grind. The same ol' same ol'—whatever you want to call it, a lot of people are looking for a way out. Many today have a sense that their lives are not their own, that they have few choices and little power over their own destinies. They see their lives getting away from them, moving at a frantic pace they feel powerless to control. They feel trapped in the rat race—forcing themselves, day after day, to do work they find neither meaningful nor fulfilling.

We have been told that the rat race is the road to success. Yet many today have an idea of success different from those of previous generations. For these people, success is not defined exclusively in economic terms but includes the opportunity to express their innate talents and abilities, to be creatively engaged (not simply to show up), to feel as though they are making a meaningful difference, and to integrate their spiritual values with the everyday business of working and making a living. Moreover, today there is a growing realization that an unhappy experience at work has profound psychological and social costs.

Whenever the expectations of an individual or a society significantly change, in time, their practical experience begins to transform to reflect that change. The example of romantic love illustrates the profound effect that a change in expectation can have upon the entire fabric of society. Where once people accepted being told whom they should marry and tried to make the best of it, today, they expect to marry for love. Where once people were willing to do the work they were born into, or later, following the Industrial Revolution, were content to view work merely as a means to making a living, today, many people are looking for considerably more.

A growing number of people are expecting to find a place for their heart and soul in their work, a place to express their unique talents and abilities. They want a greater sense of joy and meaning in their work. While growing rapidly, this group is, to be sure, still a minority of workers. Yet all great social movements begin with minorities, courageous pioneers who blaze trails that the less adventurous are later able to tread.

It isn't surprising that most don't expect to spend their lives doing work they love. Even in the United States, a land where social mobility has been achieved as easily as in any, one need go back only a few generations in most people's ancestry to find peasants or serfs. A peasant could never expect to choose his profession, let alone look forward to a life of creative self-expression. Even among the aristocracy, the traditional expectation in work was one of fulfilling a social role rather than of creatively expressing oneself. With the rise of the middle class, career options expanded for most people, yet work came to be seen principally as a commodity to be traded in exchange for a living. The emphasis was on securing the best exchange, not on the nature or quality of the work itself. For most people, then, the idea that they could spend their days doing work they love comes as something new. It has, for example, never been an essential part of that social ideal called the "American Dream."

The American Dream evolved from one of personal and religious freedom in the seventeenth and eighteenth centuries to one of political and economic freedom in the nineteenth and twentieth centuries. Today, the American Dream has become a global dream and, in certain respects, a global nightmare. One can only hope that in the twenty-first century, that dream will evolve to include creative freedom. There are signs that this may be the case, but it is still far too early to tell.

The redefinition of work will be one of the great tests of human creativity in the twenty-first century. It has been estimated that 75 percent of all jobs involve the kind of repetitive functions that can be replaced by computers or machines. In the economically developed nations, new technologies and the exportation of jobs to the "developing nations" have meant the elimination of millions of jobs. In the Third World, the introduction of large-scale farming has pushed and will likely continue to push billions into the cities, where there are too few jobs and inadequate infrastructure and housing to absorb them humanely.

Unless we are to face global unemployment on a truly horrific scale or the prospect of a virtual slave class of low-paid workers, new kinds of work must be created. This new work will not be created by the government, but neither will it come from the private sector, if we mean by that the massive global corporations. It will be created, if at all, by individuals. It will be born of their inspirations, compassion, and natural talents.

The problem is not so much one of "putting people to work" as it is of empowering them to work—unleashing and not repressing their innate creative powers. This process begins with each individual finding the work he or she loves. While the idea of doing the work you love may be new to some, it harkens back to a cardinal tenet of many sacred and philosophical traditions—namely, that each of us is called to do a unique life's work. This book is written in the hope that it may, in some way, help you to hear that call.

How to Find the Work You Love

Chapter 1

The Work You Love Is Calling

Everyone has been made for some particular work and the desire for that work has been put in his {or her} heart. — RUMI

The quest for the work you love—it all begins with the two simple questions: Who am I? and What in the world am I doing here? While as old as humanity itself, these perennial questions are born anew in every man and woman who is privileged to walk upon this earth. Every sane man or woman, at some point in his or her life, is confronted by these questions—some while but children; more in adolescence and youth; still more at midlife or when facing retirement; and even the toughest customers at the death of a loved one or when they themselves have a brush with death. Yes, somewhere, sometime, we all find ourselves face to face with the questions, Who am I? and What am I here for?

And we do make some attempt to answer them. We ask our parents and teachers, and it seems they do not know. They refer us to political and religious institutions, which often crank out canned answers devoid of personal meaning. Some even tell us that life has no meaning, save for eating and breeding. Most of us are smart enough to recognize that canned answers or begging the question will not do. We must find real answers for ourselves. But that takes more heart and effort than we are often willing to give.

What becomes of us? We get swallowed up in the rat race. Trapped. Before we have even begun in earnest the quest to find our own answers, we resign ourselves to lives without meaning. Once in this dreary and monotonous chase, it takes more courage than most of us can muster to stand up amidst the crowd and return to the quest for a fully integrated life. We sell out the ancient quest, contenting ourselves with bread, bed, and trinkets. Wordsworth warned, "Getting and spending, we lay waste our powers"—but like lemmings running headlong to the sea, we are oblivious.

We give up the quest and shove the questions into a closet deep in the back of our minds. Once in a while, a wind blows through our lives, and the closet door swings open. We battle against the wind to close it once again. Frightened by what lies behind the door, we exhaust ourselves in the effort to keep it shut. Unanswered life questions are the real skeletons in our closets. Far more than by our dreadful deeds, we are haunted by these unanswered questions: Who am I? and What am I to do here? We dare not be alone too long without some diversion, lest their bones begin to rattle.

But not all are as frail as this. Some stand tall and embrace these questions in the broad light of daily experience. Some even succeed in answering for themselves these perennial questions. They are the ones who experience deep meaning and joy in life—they are the ones who find the work they love.

The Work You Love: Your Natural Vocation

If our true nature is permitted to guide our life, we grow healthy, fruitful, and happy.   —ABRAHAM MASLOW

In all likelihood, you picked up this book because *you* are interested in finding the work you love. Of course, in order to find anything, it helps to have a clear idea of what you are looking for. Throughout this book, we will refer to the work you love as *your life's work*. Your life's work is the work you were born to do—the most appropriate vehicle through which to express your unique talents and abilities. More than a job or career, it is your special gift to humanity. Traditionally, life's work was called *vocation*, a word which literally means "calling." The work you love—your calling, or life's work—is your unique and living answer to the question, What am I here to do on this earth?

While each of us must chart our own path on the road to life's work, we should recognize that there is much to learn from those who have traveled it before. Vocational

3

choice is an issue that has occupied many of the world's great spiritual, artistic, and intellectual leaders. We cannot read the writings of Aristotle, the sayings of Confucius, or the teachings of the Buddha, the Bible, Koran, or Bhagavad-Gita without sooner or later encountering a theory of vocational choice. The world's great spiritual and philosophical traditions have long recognized the central role that vocational choice plays in the total health and happiness of the individual and in the vitality and character of a culture.

It is not difficult to understand why. Perhaps nothing says more about us as individuals than what we do; certainly, nothing reveals as much about our character as *why* we do it; and taken together, our vocational choices determine the quality of life on this planet.

While vocational choice has long been recognized as a defining moment in the life of the individual and critical to the character of a culture, it has become, if anything, even more important in the modern world. Historically, vocational or career choice was available only to a relative few—the social, artistic, and intellectual elites in isolated urban centers. The great mass of people lived traditional agrarian or nomadic lifestyles, where little changed from century to century. Even in the great cities of the ancient world, many people were slaves or limited by class or caste in the work they could do. For most people, then, vocational choice simply was not an issue; they would expect to do what their parents before them had done.

Early in the twenty-first century, for the first time in human history, most of the people on this planet will live not in traditional rural settings but in modern urban ones, which offer at least the promise of a wide range of vocational options. Add to this the unprecedented size of the world's population, and we can quickly see that today, vocational choice is a critical global issue—if for no other reason than that it affects the daily lives of billions of human beings. Moreover, with more people making vocational choices than ever before, the social and environmental impact of these choices has increased dramatically. Unless we begin to factor into our career choices a sense of our responsibility to the environment and the human community, continued environmental degradation and social disintegration are inevitable.

Certainly, the need for the wisdom reflected in the traditional understanding of vocational choice has never been greater; yet it has been all but forgotten amidst the hubbub of modern commercial culture. We have become fixated on the economic value of work to the exclusion of virtually all other values. Perhaps the simplest way of illustrating this is to consider what is generally regarded as a good job. For most people today, a good job means good pay, good benefits, and security. Little is said about the content or the quality of the work itself, let alone about the joy of expressing one's unique talents or the sense of meaning that comes from serving others.

When we contrast the prevailing notion of career success with any of a number of traditional theories of vocational choice, the modern view seems one-dimensional and shallow. Traditional theories of vocation were not necessarily more complicated, but they did reflect a deeper and more mature philosophy. Consider as an example of traditional vocational theory a simple formula given by the Greek philosopher Aristotle. He said, "Where your talents and the needs of the world cross, there lies your vocation." This simple statement tells you everything you need to know to find the work you love.

Like any theory for making vocational choice, it reflects a philosophy of life—a set of values. In the final analysis, we cannot answer the question, What am I here to do? without in some way answering the question, Who am I? For example, when we select pay, benefits, and job security as the key criteria for vocational choice, we are reflecting a set of values (whether we are conscious of it or not) that equates the individual quest for material comfort with the ultimate purpose of human existence. The implicit assumption is that human happiness and material comfort are one and the same. On the other hand, to suggest that when making vocational choices, we ought to look for an intersection between our individual talents and the needs of the world implies that human happiness springs from individual creative expression and meaningful participation in the life of society.

Within Aristotle's simple formula, there lies a profound understanding of human nature. In effect, he is saying that because we are social beings, we ought to look to, become aware of, and identify the needs of the world; and because we are individuals, we ought to look to, become aware of, and identify our own unique talents. Furthermore, he is suggesting that these two elements of our nature not only can but in fact *ought to* be in harmony.

The decision as to what your career is to be is a very deep and important one, and it has to do with something like a spiritual requirement and commitment. —JOSEPH CAMPBELL

As social beings, our interest in the needs of the world is not a matter of doing good for others out of a sense of largess. It's a matter of being true to ourselves. It comes with recognizing that, as Herman Mellville put it, "we cannot live only for ourselves. A thousand fibers connect us with our fellow-men; and along those fibers, as sympathetic threads, our actions run as causes, and they come back to us as effects." In the end, we *are* the world, and our individual choices, taken together, create the world

7

we live in. The work of creating a better world begins not with government programs or revolutionary movements but with the thoughts, feelings, and actions of individuals.

As individuals, we each comprise a unique constellation of talents, abilities, and innate interests. Working in a way that takes advantage of our unique talents, abilities, and interests means working *with* our strengths. Many people spend their whole lives working *against* their strengths—doing work not really suited to their abilities. The key is to find the work you were born to do—the one that takes full advantage of your special talents, interests, and abilities. This brings not only greater effectiveness but greater joy. On the other hand, to fail to express your own talents is not only to deny your individuality, but to withhold from the world those special gifts which you possess.

We cannot, then, separate our philosophy of life from the practical choices we make about career. If we make our career choices solely or even primarily on the basis of material comfort and then complain that the world is too commercial, that people are too selfish, that our cultural life is bland and lacking creative vitality—it is simply because we have failed to recognize that we *are* the world. We are asking others to live by a standard we ourselves have failed to embrace.

Ultimately, the discovery of a life's work begins with the realization of what it means to be a human being—

embracing what binds us all together and appreciating what makes each of us unique. As long as we deny that we are social beings and ignore the needs of the world, we miss the sense that our work is meaningful. We feel cut off, lonely, and alienated. As long as we deny our individuality and fail to develop and express our unique talents and gifts, we miss the joy of creative self-expression. We feel frustrated, repressed, and trapped. Simply put: *To the extent that your work takes into account the needs of the world, it will be meaningful; to the extent that through it you express your unique talents, it will be joyful.*

The quest for the work you love—it all begins with a few simple questions: Who am I? What in the world am I doing here? What is my special gift to give? Where it ends is up to you. To be satisfying, your answers must be more than mere philosophical speculation; they must become your life. Any philosophy, no matter how high-minded or grand, crumbles like a castle in the sand unless its principles are applied in everyday life. Doing the work you love means living your philosophy. It means putting your values to work by determining to make what you do reflect who you really are.

The First of All Problems

It is the first of all problems for a man {or woman} to find out what kind of work he {or she} is to do in this universe.
— THOMAS CARLYLE

Finding out what work we are to do in this universe— Thomas Carlyle called this "the first of all problems." It isn't difficult to understand why. The typical person will spend more of his or her adult life working than doing anything else. It is through our work, more than in any other way, that we express ourselves and participate in the life of society. Moreover, since it occupies so much of our time, energy, and attention and is so critical to our sense of psychological well-being and social fulfillment, the quality of our work experience deeply affects other areas of our lives. Finally, it is through our work that we receive the financial support necessary not only for survival but for the full enjoyment of life. We will briefly explore each of these aspects: work and the time of your life, work and the meaning of life, work and the rest of your life, and work and the riches of life.

Work and the Time of Your Life

My employer uses twenty-six years of my life for every year I get to keep. And what do I get in return . . . for my life?

— MICHAEL VENTURA

Have you ever stopped to consider how much of your life is going into work? If you are like most people, nothing will occupy more of your waking adult life. Consider what becomes of the 168 hours you have each week. Today in America, a typical adult works 8 hours a day, 5 days a week. In addition, we average another 1 1/2 hours daily in preparation and travel time. American adults sleep an average of 7 1/2 hours each night. If you add the work, preparation, and sleep time, you get 103 out of 168 hours. That leaves just 65 waking hours per week for anything other than work. Thirty-three, or more than half, of the remaining hours are on the weekend. That means that on weekdays, the typical person has little over 6 hours a day for anything other than work. An hour per meal leaves less than 3 1/2 remaining hours.

Since the great majority of people find neither deep meaning nor real joy in their work, it is hardly surprising that we have developed a popular fantasy called "living for the weekends." Weekends are the only time most people feel free to do what they want. Yet weekends and vacations comprise only a tiny fraction of the hours we invest in work. Spending most of your life doing something you don't enjoy or believe in to buy a little freedom on the weekends seems a terrible bargain indeed. As Joseph Campbell put it, "I think the person who takes a job in order to live—that is to say, [just] for the money—has turned himself into a slave."

On the other hand, in the words of R. G. Collingwood: "Perfect freedom is reserved for the man who lives by his own work and in that work does what he wants to do." Since you probably spend more waking hours working than doing anything else, your work must be something that you can be proud of, be creative in, and enjoy—if you are to have a happy and fulfilling life.

Work and the Meaning of Life

The only ones among you who will be really happy are those who have sought and found how to serve. —ALBERT SCHWEITZER

Somewhere along the line, we may have gotten the idea that life is for getting. We think that if we could just get more money or approval, more fame or love, everything would be terrific. As corny as it may sound, giving really is what it is all about. Tapping into your desire to give is the key to unlocking your own sense of purpose and to releasing your talents. It is the key, in other words, to finding the work you love.

Everyone wants to feel that they are making a constructive difference in the lives of others. Even the most jaded, selfish, or greedy person will offer a rationalization for how what he or she is doing is *really* helping people. In a sense, we are all already giving in some way. Yet, by focusing on our desire to serve, we increase our capacity to make a difference and grow into the best use of our lives. As Mahatma Gandhi put it, "Consciously or unconsciously, every one of us does render some service or other. If we cultivate the habit of doing this service deliberately, our desire for service will steadily grow stronger, and will make, not only for our own happiness, but that of the world at large."

Again, expressing your desire to give is the path to greater meaning and deeper joy. Think of the times when you've felt happiest and best about yourself. If you look carefully, you'll find that most of the time it was because you were in some way giving to others. Think about what you did today. Isn't it the giving that counts? Think of the movies you've seen, the novels you've read. Aren't many of the great ones about individuals learning to give and the struggles they encounter on the way to giving their gifts?

Your contributions will be what you treasure most in

the final analysis. But don't take my word for it. Go to nursing homes and listen to people who have the wisdom of age. The stories of their giving are the most memorable—the ones that bring the twinkle to their eyes and the smile to their faces, the ones that warm your heart and make you feel proud to be a human being. We find lifelong meaning in giving through the work we love.

People who are truly dedicated to their work—people like Buckminster Fuller, Albert Schweitzer, Mahatma Gandhi, Mother Theresa, and Pablo Picasso—continue to thrive on into old age. On the other hand, an inactive retirement ages people faster than the sun makes raisins out of grapes. José Ortega y Gasset put it well when he said: "An unemployed existence is a negation worse than death itself because to live means to have something definite to do . . . a mission to fulfill . . . and in the measure in which we avoid setting our life to something, we make it empty. . . . *Human life, by its very nature, has to be dedicated to something*."

Giving your gifts to others is, in a very real sense, giving to yourself. You may think you are giving to others, but you are really giving yourself a chance to be your best. You're giving yourself a chance to live your values, express your talents, and share your love. You're giving yourself a chance to experience yourself making a meaningful difference and to feel fully alive in the process. Since you spend most of your time working, isn't it worth the effort to arrange your life so that what you do to earn a living is what makes you feel best about yourself? Isn't that a gift you owe yourself?

Work and the Rest of Your Life

There are costs and risks to a program of action, but they are far less than the long range risks and costs of comfortable inaction.
—JOHN F. KENNEDY

Life is an integrated whole. We fool ourselves if we think it can be divided into discrete segments or compartments. Each area of our lives affects all the others. The unhappiness that results from a frustrating experience of work cannot be contained; it spills across the entire spectrum of our lives. On the other hand, doing the work you love promotes happiness in other seemingly unrelated areas of your life. Once you have identified the work you love and have begun taking positive steps to realize it, you can set about balancing it with other important aspects of your life.

While, in the long run, doing the work you love is critical to a balanced and harmonious life, the process of making a change in an area as fundamental as work can be disruptive. Going through the process of a career change can put significant strain on our relationships. Our loved ones may feel neglected, should we have to devote additional time to our work through a period of transition or retraining. We may have to deal with the fears and anxieties of our life partners or parents, or with their inability to see the merit in the course we are pursuing. We may have to confront, as never before, our own insecurities and self-doubt, as we leave behind the security of what we have done before and risk going after what we really want. For these and many more reasons, it may seem easier to settle for less than to take the risks and endure the temporary upheavals that accompany change. To be sure, the risks and costs of making a career change are immediate and apparent. Yet, while they may seem more remote and obscure, there are even *greater* costs associated with settling for anything less than the work you love.

The individual who continues in work that he hates, is bored with, or is merely indifferent to, or who resigns himself to being treated like a cog in a machine loses self-respect. His self-confidence evaporates. He begins to feel bitter and resentful or beaten and depressed. As Albert Camus put it, "Without work, all life goes rotten. But when work is soulless, life stifles and dies." To live your life to the fullest, you must find a way to put your heart and soul into your work. If your present work does not allow you to do this, find one that will.

When we fail to confront the unhappiness or frustration we feel in our work lives and to make the necessary changes, we may turn to self-destructive forms of escape in a vain attempt to mask or numb our pain. One who feels trapped in a hopeless and desperate work situation may seek escape through a variety of means—everything from excessive television watching and overeating, to drug or alcohol abuse, all the way to suicide. Escape may take the form of endless love affairs, as one tries to fill with admirers the void left by his failure to adequately express himself and his gifts. It may take the form of excessive spending. One may bring great anxiety upon himself and his loved ones by attempting to live far beyond his means in an attempt to impress upon himself and others that he has made it, that he is okay. Far from bringing relief, attempts to run away from the pain of one's work life inevitably inflict further damage on an individual's self-esteem. *The best course is to face the issue square on, to admit your unhappiness and begin charting a course that in time will lead to a fulfilling life's work.*

Many personal relationships have been destroyed by the failure of one or both parties to achieve a clear sense of direction or purpose in their lives. The aimless party feels badly about him- or herself and so begins to find fault with, and make excessive demands on, the other. These people demand attention, wanting the other to constantly reassure them that they are lovable and okay. This becomes a horribly destructive and draining game. We cannot demand from others what we can only earn for ourselves by committing ourselves to living up to our best. We are not here to be someone else or just to be with someone else. We're here to be ourselves, to make our unique contributions to the world.

When we are unhappy at work, we don't leave our unhappiness on the job; we carry it with us wherever we go. The frustration, resentment, or anxiety we feel in our work experience is inevitably, even if unintentionally, taken out on our loved ones. It is not only marital relationships that suffer; our relationships with our children can also be profoundly affected. The great psychiatrist Carl Jung said, "Nothing has a stronger influence psychologically on . . . children, than the unlived lives of their parents." When we fail to live up to our potential and settle for less, we are giving our children a model and a message of what life is about. We may tell them that they can do whatever they want, but our own example makes a stronger impression. We may tell ourselves that we are sacrificing for our children's sake, but the pain of our creative repression can leave them with deep psychological wounds. *Determining to live your life to the fullest, to follow your dreams and express yourself is the greatest gift you can give to those you love—and to yourself.*

For many years, it has been known that job-related stress is a major contributing factor in a wide range of diseases. It is perhaps not surprising, then, that according to the national Centers for Disease Control and Prevention, more people die at nine o'clock on Monday morning than at any other time of day or on any other day of the week. Recent studies have indicated that the greatest risk factor for fatal heart attack is not smoking, hypertension, or high cholesterol (of which we have heard a great deal)—but job dissatisfaction. Researchers at Columbia University have observed a link between coronary disease (the leading killer of American adults) and the individual's sense of control in his or her work life. These studies suggest that as you increase creative control, you reduce negative stress. Without a doubt, bottled-up creative energy is a great source of stress. Energy wants to flow. Without constructive channels for creative release, it builds up in tension and stress, endangering our emotional and physical health.

Lord Byron said: " 'Tis very certain the very desire of life prolongs it." Surgeons will tell you that the chances of survival after a difficult operation depend largely upon the patient's will to live. A strong will to live presupposes something to live for. In his book, *The Will to Live*, Dr. Arnold A. Hutschnecker concluded that "the will to live in civilized man is a combined biological and psychological drive. As long as we have something to live for, the will to live carries us through the moments of crisis which are inevitable in every life." *Committing yourself to your life's work, then, fosters good health by reducing negative stress and by strengthening your will to live.*

It is hard to feel creative in a job that you are doing just to get by. Creativity is a way of life, not a matter of chance or a mysterious force to be summoned out of the ether. If what you are doing most of the day requires no creative skill, chances are your creativity is on the way downhill. You're not going to walk in the door and suddenly be creative at home if all day you've been vegetating at work. *Your creative powers grow and develop through use; the more you are challenged, the more you grow.*

Failing to find the work you love has costs, not only to your self-esteem, relationships, health, and creativity, but to your world. As a human community, we all lose when people's creative abilities do not find expression in constructive, purposeful action. We lose in terms of needless human suffering and untapped human potential. Around the globe, useless, even degrading work steals the spirit and saps the joy from the lives of millions, while much necessary work goes undone. Giving your gifts benefits the world, not only through the direct contributions you make and the joy you radiate, but through the living example you provide others of what is possible for them. *Determine to play your part in creating the kind of world you want to live in.*

Work and the Riches of Life

If you love and serve man, you cannot, by any hiding or stratagem, escape remuneration. —EMERSON

Sadly, today, we too often put concerns about financial security ahead of our creative passion. Ironically, many people discover that when they shake off their fears about money and commit themselves to doing the work they truly love, they begin to experience a prosperity greater than they have ever known before. They *feel* richer and more prosperous, not just in monetary terms, but in every aspect of their lives. As their sense of self-esteem grows, they become open to receiving more. Because they value the contributions they are making, they feel as though they deserve to be well paid for their efforts. As their sense of deservingness increases, money becomes less and less of an issue. Their entire relationship with money begins to transform when they no longer associate earning it with doing something they hate or dread, are bored with, or even just indifferent to, but with doing something they truly love and believe in.

In his book, *Getting Rich Your Own Way*, financial consultant Srully Blotnick concluded after a twenty year study of over one thousand men and women that the popular belief that "wealth can come to you only as a result of doing things you don't want to do" is without basis in fact. "Like so many other thoughts about 'how to get rich', it sounds reasonable and is flatly contradicted by the evidence. In fact, if you don't like your job, you are losing money. Lots of it."

Yet true prosperity can't be measured with dollar signs alone. It's difficult to feel really prosperous, no matter how much money we may make, if we earn it doing something we don't love and respect. Socrates said, "If a rich man is proud of his wealth, he should not be praised until it is known how he employs it." We could say as well that a man is not truly rich until he earns his wealth in a way that benefits others and expresses his own innate talents and abilities.

Joseph Campbell used the term "following your bliss" to indicate the lifelong pursuit of your creative passion. He said, "If you follow your bliss, you put yourself on a kind of track, which has been there all the while, waiting for you, and the life that you ought to be living is the one you are living." He went on to say that when you commit yourself to following your bliss, "doors begin to open for you where there were no doors and where they would not open for anyone else." While this may sound somewhat mystical, it is really a matter of trusting that the intelligence which is in all of life—the intelligence that turns the heavens, that migrates the birds, the intelligence that tells a seed when to germinate, that beats your heart and digests your food—lives inside of you and knows what to do with your life.

There is only one wisdom: to recognize the intelligence that steers all things. —HERACLITUS

The same intelligence that put the desire for a particular work in your heart has also built in a support system to help you realize it. A story from the legends of King Arthur illustrates the key to recognizing this built-in support system. At one point, the knight Sir Lancelot confronts a wide chasm which he must cross. Apparently, there is nothing but a bottomless pit of empty space between where he is and where he wants to go. Yet he discovers that when he takes a step out into this empty space, there is a kind of bridge connecting the two sides. While this bridge had been there all the time, it only became visible to him *after* he had taken his first step. In much the same way, when we take the first steps into the seemingly empty space that separates the life we are leading from the one we have imagined, we too discover that there is a kind of invisible support for us. Only *after* we have stepped out into the creative emptiness do we discover the bridges that have been there all the while waiting to help us across.

People who take the plunge, who commit themselves to going after what they really want, often receive a kind of invisible support they had no idea was there for them. They begin to attract to themselves the knowledge, relationships, and resources they require to accomplish their work. They have the sense that their lives are being guided by an intelligence larger and more comprehensive than their own reasoning or intellect. Listen to the voice of this natural intelligence and it will guide you to the road of happiness and the best use of your life. Rudyard Kipling called this voice "the inner helper." He said, "I have learned that when the inner helper is in charge, do not try to think consciously. Drift—wait—and obey."

Now, it is true that creating your life's work is not something you do overnight, and that you may have to support yourself doing other things through a period of transition. Yet if you commit yourself to a work that you truly love, in time, you will find that you begin shaping a life in which you are supported by that work.

Make the commitment to settle for nothing less than your best. As George Bernard Shaw put it, "The people who get on in this world are the people who get up and look for the circumstances they want, and, if they can't find them, make them." Are you willing to apply the effort necessary to demand of life a real sense of purpose and creative passion—the work you truly love? Or will you settle for a fearful existence haunted by the ghost of might-have-been? If you think you might be ready for the adventure of your real life's work, read on.

Chapter 2

Are You Listening?

A wise man knows that he has only one enemy—himself. This is an enemy difficult to ignore and full of cunning. It assails one with doubts and fears. —BEN HECHT

Following the traditional understanding of vocation, we have suggested that there is for each of us a work for which we are naturally suited and gifted, a life's work, or calling. We have seen that responding to this call is essential to creating a life of meaning and joy, while missing it ultimately leads to alienation and frustration. If, in fact, the work you love *is* calling, the question then becomes: Are you listening? Listening to the call of your natural vocation requires the capacity to hear the voice of your own best self and the capacity to respond effectively to it. Later, we will consider what you can do to turn up the volume on the call.

In this chapter, we will explore how you can silence some of the static or background noise that may prevent you from hearing the call in the first place. We will identify and address the voices of doubt so that you might be better able to handle them when you hear them trying to rob you of your destiny—telling you that you must settle for less. Truly, as Shakespeare said, "Our doubts are traitors and make us lose the good we oft might win, by fearing to attempt."

At times it may seem that our inner world is nothing more than an endless chorus of conflicting voices. We hear them rattling around in our heads—the voices of the media and popular culture, the voices of our parents and peers, the voices of our escapist fantasies and infantile fears. To engage the creative life, you must be able to discern the voice of your own best self amidst the clamor and confusion of this strange and bewildering cacophony. You must be able to discriminate between what is really true for you and what merely sounds good. Now, that may sound easy enough, but make no mistake—traitorous doubt is a clever foe. It knows only too well how to mask its fear behind excuses and arguments that sound altogether practical, reasonable, and logical. It knows how to stop you in your tracks before you have taken even your first step on the road to the work you love.

While doubt has an endless number of voices, the major ones with regard to creating a life's work can be grouped into four categories: doubts about your ability to make it financially, doubts about what other people will think, doubts about your own creative abilities, and doubts about taking responsibility for yourself and your world.

Becoming aware of the voices of doubt will help to inoculate you against their debilitating effects on your life. As Maurice Maeterlinck said, "It is far more important that one's life should be perceived than that it should be transformed; for no sooner has it been perceived, than it transforms itself of its own accord." Once you see these traitorous voices for what they are, you will no longer give them your ear. When you stop listening to the voices of doubt, it will be much easier to begin listening to yourself.

Voices of Doubt:	Fears About . . .	Creative Responses:
The Voice of Gloom and Doom	Financial Security	Trust Yourself
The Voice of Conformity	Straying from the Pack	Free Yourself
The Voice of Self-Diminishment	Not Being Good Enough	Express Yourself
The Voice of Idle Complaint	Taking Responsibility	Challenge Yourself

The Voice of Gloom and Doom

If you are going to let the fear of poverty govern your life . . . your reward will be that you will eat, but you will not live.

—GEORGE BERNARD SHAW

It is fear about money and economic survival that, more than anything, stops people from taking up the quest for the work they love. The Voice of Gloom and Doom tells you that you couldn't possibly do the work you love and be supported by that work. It tells you that you are lucky to have any job at all and that you had better just hunker down and hold on. It may seem risky to commit yourself to the path of meaningful and enjoyable work when those around you seem content with settling for less and you are not sure that you will be able to support yourself. Yet, like all the voices of doubt, the one that tells you that you must sell out or abandon your dreams to make a living is both a traitor and a liar. It is a traitor to your heart and a liar to your pocketbook.

The truth is that in today's economy, it is far riskier to abandon your creative passion than to follow it. The transition from the industrial to the electronic or information economy and the rise of the global marketplace has displaced millions and left many more anxious about their economic futures. They understand that they can no longer rely on their employers to provide them with jobs they can count on. For many, the golden handcuffs (the good pay, benefits, and status that once tied them to jobs they found neither enjoyable nor meaningful) have been replaced by the golden handshake. Increasingly today, the secure job is a thing of the past. The only lasting security for the individual lies in his or her ability to find or create work. Clearly, the dramatic transformations within the economy demand that we take greater control over our work lives or risk getting lost in the shuffle.

Today, we have reached a historical watershed: for the first time, there are powerful correspondences between the attitudes necessary for a self-actualizing, creative approach to work and those necessary for success in the emerging economy. Where the old (industrial) economy rewarded the great mass of people for qualities like steadiness, company loyalty, deference to authority, and a "go along to get along" attitude, the new (information) economy favors people with qualities like self-motivation, initiative, flexibility, ability to work with a team, and the capacity to learn and adapt to change. These are precisely the qualities that have always been a part of a self-actualizing or creative approach to work. And who is more likely to exhibit these qualities than people who really love and believe in their work?

In the new economy, those who pursue their creative passions will have a tremendous edge. They will have a powerful and lasting source of motivation to grow and take

29

the steps necessary to succeed. On the other hand, those who rely on their employers to take care of them may well find themselves out in the cold.

People who once thought it risky to leave a seemingly secure job to pursue what they really want are beginning to realize that, today, it is at least as risky *not* to identify and follow their dreams. They understand that they need to take a more proactive approach to career—that they are ill-advised to leave their fate in their employers' hands. They recognize the need to be creatively involved in designing, crafting, and shaping their own careers *before* they reach a state of crisis—economic or otherwise.

Our word *crisis* comes from a Greek root meaning "to decide." A crisis is what happens when we don't decide, and a crisis often compels us to make the decision to begin orienting our work lives in a new direction. A crisis could be as dramatic as an accidental brush with death, a serious illness, an alcohol or drug addiction, the death of a loved one, a divorce, or a layoff. It could come in the form of a loss of energy and enthusiasm for life, in chronic burnout or depression. Your crisis might be as subtle as a creeping sense of boredom and dissatisfaction, a gnawing feeling that there is a great deal within you that is going unexpressed —that your life is going by without you. The riskiest course is to wait until you are forced by a crisis to reexamine your life. It is far safer to commit yourself to your creative passion, to learn to trust in your own intuition, talent, and resourcefulness, and to begin building your work life around what you really want.

While they may accept that it is a good idea for others, many people doubt that it is really possible for them to earn a living doing the work they love. Whether or not it will be possible for *you* depends, in a large measure, on whether or not you believe it is possible for you. What you believe will shape what you do and don't do. It will shape the opportunities you attract or don't attract. It will determine whether or not you can recognize opportunities when they do come along and what you do with them. One thing is for sure, if you don't believe you can, the chances that you ever will are next to nil.

If you think you can or you think you can't, you are right.
—HENRY FORD

Somewhere along the line, many of us came to accept the belief that work has to be a struggle and that we can't do what we really want to do—the notion of work as a stoic duty or "the old grind." We may have learned this from our parents, our educational system, or the popular culture. However we came to this belief, if we accepted it, we probably went out and got a job on that basis. Then, each time we got paid, the belief was reinforced, becoming ever more ingrained in our brains. The internal verbalization may have gone something like this: "I didn't do what I wanted, and they paid me for it. I got rewarded! It works to not do what I want." If you have never been paid for doing work you truly love, it may be difficult for you to accept that it is possible for you ever to do so. The knowledge that thousands of people do it every day may have little impact on you if your own experience tells you something different. You may dismiss the experience of others by telling yourself that they are somehow special or more gifted than you.

If the belief that work has to be a struggle is deeply rooted in your psyche, it's a good idea to begin as soon as possible earning money doing something you *do* enjoy. Even if it's not what you consider to be your ultimate life's work, or is only part-time, or is for less money than you will be able to charge after you've had more training and experience—begin making money by doing something you enjoy. In this way, you will begin breaking down your commitment to the belief that you can't do what you want, that work must be a dull routine or a frantic struggle. You start reinforcing the belief that it is possible to do work you enjoy and be supported in and by that work. Set out after what you really want and don't settle for less. It has been wisely said that people get in trouble in this life not because they want too much but because they settle for too little.

The Voice of Conformity

To be independent of public opinion is the first formal condition of achieving anything great. —G. W. F. HEGEL

The question may have occurred to you: If following your heart and doing the work you love is really such a great idea, why aren't more people—indeed, why isn't everyone —doing it? The simplest answer is that, as things currently stand, it means going against the grain. It takes great courage and resourcefulness to go against the grain without getting crushed by the mill of public opinion. It takes, as e. e. cummings said, the courage "to be nobody-but-yourself—in a world which is doing its best, night and day, to make you everybody else, [and that] means to fight the hardest battle which any human being can fight; and never stop fighting."

After concerns about money, the next big block that holds people back from taking up the quest for their life's work is fear of breaking away from the pack. We all want to feel as though we belong. We want to fit in and act the same, even when fitting in is insane. We bury our dreams for fear of being put down. We set aside our desire to give because that's not the way most people live. We try to tell ourselves that we should be satisfied with work that is a bore; after all, Dad was, and the neighbors don't seem to want anything more.

33

Since few people are really happy in their work, the prevailing or conformist view is very negative about the possibilities. Most people are only too ready to tell you all the reasons why you should forget your dreams for yourself and your world. If you persist, you may be perceived as something of an oddball. As T. S. Eliot put it, "In a world of fugitives/The person taking the opposite direction/Will appear to be running away." Many people you know, even those closest to you, may not understand this quest of yours. While they may congratulate you when you are ultimately successful, don't expect them to be terribly supportive during the *process* of seeking and creating your life's work. Draw support and strength from those who are themselves questing or those who are already manifesting their own life's work.

Many people avoid even considering what they really want for fear of being put down by others. They have internalized the Voice of Conformity. You too may have heard this voice. It's the one that tells you that you must stay in line and follow the prescribed formula or pattern for your life. It's the one that tells you that you must spend your life doing what you "should" do instead of what you really want to do. It's the one that tells you not to expect too much—that you will only be disappointed if you try to follow your dreams. It's the one that says, "Don't rock the boat. Don't stray too far from the beaten path."

It takes courage to admit that what we are doing now,

perhaps what we have been doing for many years, is not really right for us. Often we find that we got into a particular kind of work before we really knew who we were or what we were all about. When the time came to make a career choice or take our first "real job," we may have grasped at the first thing that came along. We wanted to seem confident, as if we knew what we were doing, as if we had an answer—even if it was not coming from a very deep place. Or we told ourselves that this job or career would be only temporary, that later we would find something more suited to our talents and interests. Over the years, we may have developed a powerful investment in and commitment to a work that was haphazardly chosen and entirely inappropriate for us. Be prepared to resume the quest for the work you love. As famed management consultant Peter Drucker has said: "The probability that the first choice you make is right for you is roughly one in a million. If you decide that your first choice was the right one, chances are you are just plain lazy."

In my work as a career consultant, I have observed that men, especially, have difficulty admitting that their work life is not working for them. They endeavor to conform to the cultural stereotype of the macho man—the strong, silent type who has everything under control. They try to uphold the illusion that they have it all together, even though on the inside they may be falling apart. (This may be one reason why suicide rates are so much higher for men.) Women generally seem more willing to acknowledge their pain. Among the men who seek out my services, I see three general categories: young men or sensitive types who are not invested in the stereotype, those who come at the urging of their wives or lovers, or those who have already achieved considerable financial success.

The last group feels that having "made it" in commercial terms gives them permission to begin considering what they would really love to do and how they can have a more meaningful experience of life by giving back to others. Having succeeded at doing what they were "supposed to do," they are ready to begin considering what they want to do. Of course, it would be much easier and make for a more productive life to go after what you want right from the start.

We hear the Voice of Conformity in the familiar admonition to keep the old nose to the grindstone as well as in alluring calls to acceptable rebellion and escape. In fact, these are but two sides of the same coin. When we have not chosen our work freely, out of love and creative passion, but because we feel compelled by economic and social pressures to fulfill a particular life pattern, inner resentment and hostility are sure to follow.

The Voice of Conformity encourages us to channel this frustration and unhappiness into escape. We all know that "happy hour" begins when work ends. Sure you can't stand your job, but wait until the weekend. Or what about that two week summer vacation?—better start planning for that right away. Perhaps nothing is more absurd than watching tourists dutifully *trying* to have fun. Because we load them with the expectation of meeting all of our unfulfilled desires, vacations and holidays often disappoint.

The Voice of Conformity encourages us to define ourselves by our possessions, not by our character or contributions. As Martin Luther King, Jr., put it, "We are prone to judge success by the index of our salaries or the size of our automobiles rather than by the quality of our service and relationship to mankind." We are encouraged to buy our way to social acceptance, to channel our inner longings and aspirations into items that can be purchased with a credit card. Unhappy, frustrated people are easy marks for those selling the illusion of escape—whether packaged as a product, service, or entertainment.

The Voice of Comformity also encourages us to vent our frustration in negativism and jealousy. Many workplaces are rife with putdowns and petty jealousies. Much of the exhaustion people experience from work comes not as a result of productive effort but from the emotional drain of political infighting, negativism, and jealousy. Since it is so prevalent, we are tempted to join in the gossip, back-biting, and back-stabbing. It is well to remember that people only feel the need to put down others when they have lost respect for themselves.

Creative self-expression has no more potent or devious

an enemy than jealousy. While in its grip, we imagine that life would be somehow better if we were someone else— or at least if we had their abilities or opportunities. Yet, we are only jealous of others because we have not yet discovered how to express our *own* abilities, to recognize and seize our own opportunities. And how can we ever learn to be and express ourselves while wishing we were someone else? Jealousy may offer a moment's twisted pleasure, but in exchange it robs us of the energy and imaginative power we need to make the most of our own lives.

Whoso would be a man must be a nonconformist. —EMERSON

The truth is, until we have taken the time to discover and affirm who we really are and what we really want, we are left with only negative identities and negative passion. We define ourselves by what we are against, and so have negative, not creative, passion. We need something to rebel against or we don't feel like we exist. We need someone to rebel against or we don't feel passionate about anything. Many people spend the whole of their lives rebelling against their parents. If we have a job, we can rebel against the boss or co-workers. If we have a mate, we can rebel against him or her. If we have circumstances we don't like, we rebel against these. We are comfortable with rebelling, but fearful of creating.

The rebel without a cause is a dependent creature who must have some authority to rebel against. Should he lose one, he will find another, for the whole structure of his inner world is built on defense. He needs an enemy as an excuse to justify his own fear and cowardice. He needs some authority to distract him from his inner emptiness, his own inability to love. While he is rebelling, he is so brave, so courageous, so sure of himself. He knows that he is right, or more accurately, he knows that *they* are wrong. He is confident and sure as long as he has an "oppressor" to struggle against but hesitates when it's time to declare his own dreams or wilts when it's time to stand up for them.

You will not find the work you love by conforming to the expectations of others; neither will you find it by rebelling against them. Genuine creativity is never the result of a defensive reaction *against* this or that, it is a positive and natural outgrowth of love. No creative work or life was built on fear and defensiveness. On the contrary, as Marsilio Ficino put it, the creative "artists in each of the arts seek after and care for nothing but love."

If we are to discover our creative passion, we must take time to be alone, to get to know ourselves and what we really love. We must articulate our own values and explore our own visions. Moreover, we must continually challenge the values asserted by the popular culture and weigh these against our own sense of what is right and true. In short, we must stand up to the Voice of Conformity and assert ourselves. As Albert Camus said, "To know oneself, one should assert oneself."

The Voice of Self-Diminishment

Nothing splendid has ever been achieved except by those who dared believe that something inside them was superior to circumstance.
— JOHN BARTON

Sure, we may fear the rejection of others or the vicissitudes of the marketplace, but this is hardly the whole story, for as George Bernard Shaw so wisely put it, "Has fear ever held a man back from what he really wanted or a woman either?" We are only troubled by the disapproval of others or the trials of the marketplace when we have lost our own creative passion, when our inner world is wracked with confusion and doubt.

The Voice of Self-Diminishment tells you that you are not good enough, that you don't deserve what you really want. It tells you that you are inadequate, unequal to the task of creating the life you want to lead. It's the one that tells you that you will screw up and fall on your face, the one that reminds you of all your previous failures. It's the one sitting on your shoulder, criticizing and judging you every step of the way. People often ask me if they can ever get this monkey off their backs. Of course, there are many ways to do this. One way is simply to starve the little critter to death. Recognize that it feeds—it lives—on attention. Listening to it *and* arguing with it both give it the attention it craves. Simply ignore it and focus your attention, instead, on what you want to create. The human mind cannot think two thoughts at the same time: while you are focused on your creative visions, old mister monkey is out of luck. As Jonas Salk put it, "I have had dreams, and I have had nightmares. I overcame the nightmares because of my dreams."

It takes a great of deal of imagination and resourcefulness to find your own way in a world determined to stamp you with a cookie cutter. Colin Wilson put it like this: "Modern civilization with its mechanized rigidity is producing more outsiders than ever before—people who are too intelligent to do some repetitive job but not intelligent [resourceful] enough to make their own terms with society." Yet today, the need to find the imagination and creative intelligence to make our own terms with society has never been greater. Even if we *were* willing to settle for them, dull repetitive jobs are rapidly being replaced by advanced technologies or shipped overseas to those who will work for less.

The creative life requires the activation of the creative imagination, or what Emerson called the "active soul." He said, "The one thing in the world, of value, is the active soul." The active soul engages its creative imagination in the process of turning intangible visions into tangible realities. It is the imagination that turns notes into music, words into poetry, color into painting. It is your imagination that will show you the way to realize your dreams. As you gather information, researching fields you are interested in working in, you feed your imagination with the raw material it needs to design a strategy for realizing your life's work. Often we think we "can't" only because we haven't made the effort to research how we could. Again, focus your attention on what you want and you increase your desire to achieve it. When the desire becomes strong enough, you act. As you act, you generate a momentum of success.

You give birth to that on which you fix your mind.
—ANTOINE DE SAINT-EXUPÉRY

When our imaginations are not creatively engaged, they don't just sit idly by; they busy themselves conjuring fearful futures or escapist fantasies. People wonder why they are so "uncreative," why it is that their own souls are not possessed with the fire of creative inspiration they have seen in the lives of others. Human beings are naturally creative; yet to expect our imaginations to be constructively engaged while they are busy recycling a monotonous and wearisome round of worries and fantasies is surely asking too much.

If my imagination is preoccupied with worries and silly fantasies, how can I ever hear the voice of my true self calling me to a life of creative adventure? How can I ever know the kind of desire or creative passion that transcends fear? One whose soul is active is free to let her imagination wander in a creative quest. She is free to seek a vision of her destiny and, having found it, free to fix her attention on the creative visions she has seen.

The great dancer and choreographer Martha Graham described the creative process as a mixture of terror and joy. The *terror* is the fear of not being able to render the thing imagined in the world of time and space. The discrepancy between the vision or ideal and the manifest reality goes with the territory of the creative life. The manifested thing or event is never as perfect as the vision that inspired it. Actual paintings, poems, or performances, as beautiful as they may be, never quite match the ones seen in the artist's mind. Vincent Van Gogh concurred with fellow painter Cyprien's observation that "the most beautiful pictures are those one dreams about when smoking pipes in bed, but which one will never paint."

People who tend to be perfectionists are often terrified to the point of procrastination and paralysis by the prospect of failing to achieve the ideal. They are too impatient and self-critical, becoming frustrated and discouraged if they don't get it right on the first try. People in touch with their creativity accept imperfection, keep their fear in check, and forge ahead—striving always for their best work, yet realizing they will never quite hit the target. So much for the terror!

The *joy* is in the creative process itself—the self-abandonment in creative engagment, where the soul takes flight and leaves behind the realm of time and space. What Isabel Allende has said about writing applies to the creative process in general: "Writing is like making love: Don't worry about the orgasm, just worry about the process." Don't judge yourself for being so far from where you want to be; engage the creative process and trust that in time it will take you where you want to go. Throw yourself into the process of creating the life you want to live and let the orgasms sneak up on you.

The Voice of Idle Complaint

This is a world of action, and not for moping and groaning in.
—CHARLES DICKENS

The final voice which may distract us from our life's work is the Voice of Idle Complaint. Whether we spend our time complaining about our own situation or the state of the world, it drains off vital energy that we need to realize our dreams. It takes great energy to live a creative life. Perhaps, like many people, you wonder where you are going to get the energy you will need to realize your life's work. A good place to start is with energy conservation, or should we say, redirection. Idle complaint may be the most costly of all energy drains—complaining about your own circumstances, complaining about the faults of others, complaining about the world we live in. Too often, we confuse complaining with taking responsibility for doing something about the problems that confront us.

Idle complaint is born of a dependent, infantile psychology. It is always waiting for someone to come along—be our mommy or daddy—and make everything all better. After all, when we were infants, we had only to cry and complain and the "big people" attended to our every need. Whether it is our personal problems or the great global issues, we want "them" (the big people) to fix it for us.

Idle complaint always carries blame and a sense of helplessness with it. We blame the "big people" for not fixing things and complain that we are helpless—just one "little" person. Blaming and complaining is for babies—and for losers. Think of a sporting contest. Is it the winning or losing team that whines, blames, or comes up with excuses?

Because it originates in a psychology of helplessness, complaint inevitably leads to feelings of hopelessness and defeat. While we remain in this infantile psychological state, we actually believe that complaining will help. Yet, since we are no longer children but grown adults, there is no longer anyone dedicated to solving our problems for us.

45

Consequently, *the more we complain, the more hopeless we feel.* After all, we have done everything we know how to do (that is, we have complained and complained), yet things have not improved. We conclude that the situation must be beyond remedy.

The infantile tendency toward idle complaint has been given a certain intellectual validity though popular interpretations of the theories of Sigmund Freud and Karl Marx. Freudianism taught us to blame our parents, and Marxism, to blame the social system. Of course, our parents were far from perfect; yet if we continue to blame them, we siphon off vital energy we need to create with. Likewise, the social system is filled with flaws; yet if we blame the system, we deplete our own creative energy. We may claim that the psychological wounds inflicted by our parents or the evils of the social system keep us from realizing what we want in life. These are popular excuses, and if we take them for our own, many will accept them as legitimate. Still, this will not give us what we want in life. We may have good excuses, but we will not have what we want. Despite the traumas of your childhood and the injustices and absurdities of the social system, you can be and express yourself.

We outgrow idle complaint as we come to accept responsibility for ourselves and our world. Creative discontent comes to replace idle complaint. As much as idle complaint, creative discontent is dissatisfied with things as they are. The difference is that creative discontent is prepared to do something about it, to put its actions where its mouth is. It goes beyond mere protest and complaint and accepts the responsibility to create. It is not simply "against"; it has something to live for.

Things do not get better by being left alone.
— WINSTON CHURCHILL

It's easy to be against all the problems in the world, to speak with horror, shock, and outrage at the mess "they" have made of things. We are against poverty, injustice, and oppression. Being against these evils usually consists of condemning them at cocktail parties, coffeehouses, and dinner-table conversations. Because they are universally condemned, it takes little courage to say we are against them. On the contrary, we get strokes for it. It makes us feel good to be against all these bad things, and it takes so little effort. We just say so and let it go.

When we sell out in our daily lives, we may try to comfort ourselves and assuage our guilt by making a point of being against all the right things. Perhaps we condemn the bad things to show ourselves and others how good we are. Perhaps we feel it lets us off the hook, as though our responsibility to our fellow man has been fulfilled because we have given lip service to his ills. The problems of the world involve real pain suffered by real people. Solving them requires more than joining in the chorus of condemnation. It requires that we make the effort to understand and the effort to act. Casual conversation about social issues is meaningful when it serves to deepen understanding or to inspire positive action. Otherwise, it simply depletes the oxygen in the room.

To believe that what has not occurred in history will not occur at all, is to argue disbelief in the dignity of man.

—MAHATMA GANDHI

Can we justify complaints about the world's leaders if we are not willing to assume the responsibilities of leadership ourselves? Can we complain about the greed of individuals or corporations when we ourselves are too greedy to sacrifice even a little of our time to make the world a better place? Can we complain about the ignorance and selfishness of people whom we have made no effort to educate, for whom we have provided no example of a better way? Can we complain that we hate our jobs when we have made no effort to identify what we really want, or have given up too easily on realizing it?

We know what we are against, but what are we for? What positive visions inspire our hearts? How much effort do we put into creating the kind of world we want to live in? While it is popular and easy to be *against*, being *for* can be controversial and far more difficult. When you suggest a positive alternative, people may take potshots at you or tell you all the reasons why it won't work. They may laugh at you, call you "silly," "idealistic," or "fanatic," or put roadblocks in your way. The cocktail complainer risks none of these. He says, "I'm against all the right things. Please pass the cheese." He'll be safe, free from criticism and reproach, accepted, smug, and superior to the bad guys who are politically incorrect. We get strokes for being passively against and criticized or attacked for what we stand up for. It's easy, then, to see why more people aren't willing to take responsibility for their world. It takes courage and self-confidence. It takes believing in humanity and in yourself.

Believing in Humanity and in Yourself

Few will have the greatness to bend history itself, but each of us can work to change a small portion of events.

—ROBERT KENNEDY

Love gives us the courage to believe in humanity and in ourselves. The word *courage* means, literally, "with heart." It takes great heart—great courage—to believe in humanity in the face of what sometimes seem like overwhelming problems. It takes courage to affirm that the possible world that many of us have experienced in glimpses, moments of imagination or spiritual insight, is more than an idle fantasy. It takes the courage to say, like Martin Luther King, Jr., "I have a dream"—to affirm against all evidence to the contrary that one day, *we shall overcome* our fear, doubt, hatred, violence, and pettiness. It takes courage to commit yourself to building bridges between the world that could be and the world that is—the courage to say that you believe the world will one day be a better place and that today you are ready to do your part to make it so.

Many people refuse even to acknowledge their dreams for the world because they believe they can't make a difference. They will tell you that it's arrogant or foolish to imagine that *you* can make a difference. After all, who are you? Just one small person in a sea of humanity. You're not a leader or a famous personality. You have no following or power base. What good are you going to do anyway? You're just kidding yourself, being a do-gooder.

On the other hand, many "do-gooders" have given doing good a bad name because of their self-righteousness, ulterior motives, lack of commitment, ignorance of the values and needs of the people they are serving, and the like. You can't save the world. But you *can* do what you can, and you do it because you can—not to save the world, but just because you can. While no one of us can single-handedly alter the direction of society, neither can any of us ignore the impact that our choices have on the world. As Mother Teresa puts it, "What we do is only a drop in the ocean, but if we didn't do it, the ocean would be one drop less."

It is, of course, a challenge to do what's right without becoming self-righteous: to remain open-minded, tolerant of other points of view, responsive to the needs of the people you're serving, and aware of the concerns of those who may be in opposition to you. Still, that is the challenge. Far from producing feelings of self-righteousness or arrogance, genuine loving service produces the feelings of tolerance and deep humility seen in people like Mahatma Gandhi, Mother Teresa, and Martin Luther King, Jr. Don't worry. If your vision is of a world of peace and justice, brotherhood and freedom—and you take responsibility for creating it—you probably won't have cause for arrogance in the foreseeable future.

To creatively engage your life's work, you must not only believe in the human potential; you must believe in yourself. In today's psychological jargon, believing in yourself is called having "high self-esteem." Textbook descriptions aside, high self-esteem can be defined by two little words: *I can.* As a practical matter, improving your self-esteem means expanding the scope and difficulty of activities to which you respond with the confident words "I can." I can create a way. I can learn. I can manage. I can communicate. I can concentrate. I can persist. I can be victorious.

Some people have difficulty identifying their life's work because low self-esteem prevents them from believing that they could ever make a real difference in the lives of others. Negative self-image obscures and distorts their view of themselves. Through this veil they are unable to recognize their special talents and gifts, their intrinsic dignity and worth. If you find yourself in this group, recognize that there are many things you can do to raise your self-esteem. Foremost among these is to make your life about giving to others. As you see yourself helping people, you experience your basic goodness, dignity, and worth. Your own behavior makes a liar out of the inner voices of doubt. Even if you think yourself unworthy of a genuine purpose or mission in life, give what you can (or rather, what you think you can). The more you give, the more you'll know that you can give more.

In one respect, self-esteem is earned through effort and experience. Yet self-confidence isn't based upon mere history alone. There is a difference between an *I can* that comes out of having done the thing before and an *I can* that comes out of having faith that you can do it. A general belief in yourself will count the most when it's time to put your vision into action, for you may have to do many things you have never done before.

The future belongs to those who believe in the beauty of their dreams.   —ELEANOR ROOSEVELT

Self-confidence is required to dream your dream for a better world and to believe that you can play your part to make it a reality. Whether we like it or not, confident people shape the world. They are the doers, movers, and shakers. Confident people with good character (life-affirming values) make the world a better place. Confident people with not-so-good character make the world a worse place. Hitler and Stalin had confidence, to be sure; but so did Gandhi, Martin Luther King, Jr., and Mother Teresa. The timid watch from the sidelines of life while those with confidence battle it out. Because they put their beliefs into action, confident people determine the values of their societies. Remember, as La Rochefoucauld said, "Nothing is so contagious as an example. We never do great good or great evil without bringing about more of the same on the part of others."

As we have seen, embracing the work you love means making a lifelong commitment to yourself. It means deciding to trust the voice of your own best self and to honor your deepest desires. In the remainder of this book, we will focus on some specific strategies for tapping into the work you love. Now, if you are ready to turn a deaf ear to the voices of doubt, to listen to the angels of your better nature and act on their inspirations, read on. A new day dawns for you if you have the courage to go out and meet it.

Chapter 3

Heeding the Call

Look within. Within is the fountain of good, and it will ever bubble up, if thou wilt ever dig. —MARCUS AURELIUS

We have seen that we can't answer the question, What am I here to do? without at the same time answering the question, Who am I? Moreover, we have seen the need to become aware of and turn from the voices of doubt that would otherwise drown out the call to life's work. Now, we will explore a variety of ways in which you can tap into or discover your life's work. Where will you find the work you love? Ultimately, you will find it deep within yourself. It's not something you make up or figure out, but an integral part of yourself that you uncover—not something you add to yourself, but something that you draw out from within. Even as a plant grows toward the light, you will naturally grow toward the work you love, once you have identified it and committed yourself to it.

While engaged in the process of finding the work you love, it will help if you begin with the assumption that it really is possible for you to become aware of, and ultimately to do, the work that is right for you. Give yourself permission to dream, imagine, and explore—to really open up to yourself and discover what's "in there."

The process of finding the work you love is best understood as a matter of making three decisions. It requires that you (1) decide what you are looking for, (2) decide to keep looking until you find it, and (3) decide when you have found it. Recognize that the "it" that you are looking for is not a career role per se. Neither is it a position or title. It is not something to *be* (the thing to be is yourself!) but something to *do*, to express, to give. What "it" is, is your creative passion, the work you were born to do. Over the course of a lifetime, it may take a variety of forms, roles, or structures; yet running through all of these will be a common thread of meaning and joy.

To Find the Work You Love:

- Decide what you are looking for.
- Decide to keep looking until you find it.
- Decide when you have found it.

Decide What You Are Looking For

Despite several decades of research, the most effective way to predict vocational choice is simply to ask the person what he wants.

—JOHN HOLLAND

Finding the work you love begins with asking the right questions. You will find no tests in this book. Though widely used, vocational tests have shown themselves to be, in many respects, inadequate and unreliable tools for making vocational choices of any kind. When it comes to finding the work you love, they are entirely inadequate. As Richard Nelson Bolles, author of the career classic *What Color Is Your Parachute?* has written, "No tests or other instruments have been devised yet that so effectively measure what you want as just asking you or having you ask yourself."

Inviting you to ask yourself what you want is precisely what we will be doing throughout the remainder of this book. You will have the opportunity to approach this question from a number of different angles, through a series of questions that will help you to identify the work you love. If you want to get the most out this book, take the time to write your answers to the focusing questions that appear at the end of sections throughout the remaining chapters.

Before we explore any new questions, it is useful to stop and consider that you have already been asking yourself questions regarding work. As you become aware of these questions, you will, in all likelihood, discover that you have answered them. (I have been inviting clients to do this exercise for many years and have yet to find anyone who has not answered the questions they have made most important, that is, the ones they have acted on.) This knowledge is empowering. For if you have answered the questions you have already asked, you can have confidence that by asking new questions, you are on your way to finding new answers.

When they begin to examine their motives, some people discover that they came to the work they now find themselves in because they were asking the question, What do my parents want me to do? Their parents' desires may have been explicitly stated (e.g., become a lawyer or doctor) or more subtly communicated (don't major in *that;* you will never find a job). What do my parents want me to do? is not a particularly good question to ask when looking for your life's work. You do not live to please others, but to become yourself. Consider: Isaac Newton's mother wanted him to run the family farm. Joseph Campbell's father wanted him to take over the family business. Dvořák's father wanted his son to follow in his footsteps and become a butcher, while Handel's father wanted him to pursue a career in law. What a waste it would have been if any of these had acceded to their parents' wishes. They would have deprived the world of their wonderful gifts.

Others recognize that they came to their current jobs because they were asking the question, What will be most in demand? They may have determined to become nurses, engineers, or computer programmers because they were told that these careers would be in high demand. They never stopped to consider whether or not these were things they would really love to do. Again, What will be in demand? is not a good question to ask if you are looking for the work you love. A life's work is created from the inside out, from your innate talents and interests, not by holding your finger up to the wind. Moreover, because of the dynamic nature of today's economy, basing your career choice on this question can often turn out to be a cruel joke. Many people spend thousands of dollars and many years of their lives training for professions they have been told will be in demand, only to discover that by the time they have completed their education, this career is no longer "hot."

Some people landed in their current careers because they were asking the question, How can I achieve power, status, and prestige? For others, it may have been, What kind of career will allow me to achieve fame or celebrity? or What kind of career will bring me the greatest income? Still others were asking questions like, What kind of work will have the fewest hassles? or What will be the least threatening and cause me to take the fewest risks? For others, questions like, What is available? or What will allow me to pay the bills? may have been central. There are those whose entire career quest amounted to asking the question, What is in the newspaper?

Now if chasing after the answers to any of these questions has given you a satisfying and fulfilling life's work, it is purely a matter of dumb luck or some kind of divine intervention. Often we get what we ask for and then complain that it is not what we want. You wouldn't go to a restaurant, order hash and then complain when they bring you hash that it is not a gourmet meal. You understand that there is a relationship between what you are asking for and what you are getting. Whether we care to admit it or not, it works the same way in our lives generally and with respect to our work in particular.

We may spend a great deal of time and energy wishing that things were different or hoping for them to get better. Yet it is unlikely that our lives will significantly improve until we assume total responsibility for where we are now. Recognize that you have arrived in your current circumstances because of the decisions you have or have not made, because of the actions you have or have not taken. Making new decisions and following them up with action gives you the power to change your life.

Sometimes we think we have no answers when the real problem is that we haven't asked the right questions. It is well to remember that, as Einstein said, "the formulation of a problem is more important than the solution." If we want a joyous and meaningful experience of work, we must

59

begin asking the questions appropriate to this. We might start by asking questions such as:

- What was I born to do? or What is my destiny?
- What would be my greatest contribution to others? or What gifts do I want to share?
- What would I really love to do? What is my natural work? or What are my talents?
- What is the best use of my life? or What am I ready to dedicate myself to?

In a sense, all of these are really the same question. The work that you truly love to do is the work you were born to do, will be your greatest contribution to others, and will demand the very best from you.

A study of the lives of those recognized for making outstanding contributions reveals that many had the benefit of a central question that guided their lives, a life-informing question that they kept in the forefront of their minds. For example, Martin Luther King, Jr., said, "Life's most urgent question is, What are you doing for others?" —and we can see that his life became his answer to this question. Joseph Campbell chose as his life-guiding question, "Where is my bliss?" It led him to the study of mythology, which he helped to reinvigorate and popularize in the later part of the twentieth century.

When framing your central question, tailor it to your

individual needs and be as specific as you like. For example, in seeking his calling, Buckminster Fuller asked: "What —if anything—[could] a healthy young male human of average size, experience, and capability with an economically dependent wife and newborn child, starting without capital or any kind of wealth, cash savings, account monies, credit, or university degree . . . effectively do that could not be done by great nations or great private enterprise to lastingly improve the physical protection and support of all human lives, aboard our planet Earth?"

We could give many more examples from the lives of famous people; yet this technique is not a prerogative of the "greats." I have seen the power that comes from framing a central life question at work in the lives of many not-so-famous people who, in their own ways, have realized greatness. In your own words and in a way that is meaningful to you, frame a question that works for you. Decide what you are looking for!

Focusing Questions

• Write down your present occupation or, if you are unemployed, your previous occupation. Now take a few minutes to write down the question you were asking that led you into this occupation. For example: What will bring in the most money? What will take the least effort? What is most in demand? What will please my parents? What will gain me status and prestige? What will be the most secure? What is listed in the newspaper?

- Since you are reading this book, we will assume that you are interested in changing your work experience and, therefore, in asking a new question. Now write the question that you want to use to shape the remainder of your work life. Make sure that it is really meaningful to you. Here are some examples of questions that others have selected. What would I really love to do? What was I born to do? How can I be useful? What is my natural work? What would give me the greatest joy and satisfaction?

Decide to Keep Looking Until You Find It

It is important to recognize that all of the famous people we mentioned above not only made the decision to become conscious of what they were looking for, to frame a central life-informing question; they also made a second decision. They decided to stay with it until they had found answers that were meaningful to them. Sometimes we imagine that the greats of history were always clear about what to do with their lives, that they never had to wrestle with doubt or uncertainty. This is a big mistake, as reading their biographies clearly shows.

Once you decide what *you* are looking for, determine to persist until you find it. Many of us have not learned to claim or assert what we want, not only in terms of career, but in other areas of our lives as well. It may take us some time before we are ready to admit that we do, in fact, know what we want. Be patient with yourself. As the poet Rainer Maria Rilke put it, "Be patient toward all that is unsolved in your heart and . . . try to love the *questions themselves*. . . ."

Decide When You Have Found It

The final and most important decision in the process of finding the work you love is the decision that you have found what you are looking for. This means to definitely and unequivocally claim that you know what your work is. We are often afraid to declare what we really want because it puts us on the spot to do something about it. Yet for many, making this claim is the only step required. At some point, they have already tapped into what they are here to do on this earth. They may have then begun to overanalyze it and think of all the reasons it wouldn't work, to doubt themselves and their intuitions. Or perhaps they took some preliminary steps and gave up when things became difficult.

We should recognize that claiming the work you love can seem like a big *emotional* risk. If you have a job that is not coming out of who you really are (your creative passion), you might erect an emotional barrier between yourself and your work. Then, when your work is criticized or you fail to do your best, you can say, "Well, this is just my job. It has nothing to do with my real life." But when you are doing work you really love and are criticized or come up against doubts about your ability to see it through, you may feel much more vulnerable. It takes great courage, then, to claim that you know what you want.

Whether you already know what your life's work is or you must still go through a process of discovering it, decide that once you become aware of the work that is calling you, you will answer the call. Make your claim and trust yourself to see it through. As Epictetus said, "First say to yourself what you would be; and then do what you have to do."

I. S.E.E.: The Work I Love

The remainder of this book is organized around a simple formula indicated by the acronym I. S.E.E., which stands for the four key elements that are to be found in every genuine life's work. These are Integrity, Service, Enjoyment, and Excellence. Keep these elements in mind as you look for your own life's work. Again, the clearer you are about what you are looking for, the easier it will be to find. These keys will help you further clarify what you are looking for.

Element	Creative Power	Focusing Question
Integrity	Conscience	What speaks to me?
Service	Compassion	What touches me?
Enjoyment	Talent	What turns me on?
Excellence	Destiny	What draws out my best?

Integrity: A life's work is inspired from within, born of your own values, visions, and intuitions; it has the quality of integrity.

Service: A life's work is useful to others, providing you with the opportunity to give your gifts in a meaningful way; it has the quality of service.

Enjoyment: A life's work is natural to you, allowing you to take full advantage of your innate talents and abilities; it has the quality of enjoyment.

Excellence: A life's work prompts you to do your best work; you love what you are doing enough to do your best work; it has the quality of excellence.

It should be noted that the four elements of the I. S.E.E. formula are the affirmative antidotes to the four voices of doubt which we discussed in chapter 2. We may sell out our dreams for the promise of financial security or have the *integrity* to remain true to conscience. We may seek the approval of society or have the independence and compassion to creatively *serve* it. We may give in to fears of inadequacy or know the *enjoyment* that comes from honoring and expressing our own unique talents. We may drift into the habit of laziness and idle complaint or commit ourselves to the path of genuine *excellence*.

These four elements can also be related to Aristotle's philosophy of vocation, which we discussed in chapter 1. The elements of *integrity* and *enjoyment* reflect your individual character, your innate interests and talents. The elements of *service* and *excellence* reflect your social nature, your compassion and desire to share with others your highest quality of work. We will find that each of these elements provides powerful clues for the discovery of your life's work. Some may speak to you more powerfully than others. While it is useful to consider all of these elements, recognize that any one of them alone may guide you to the work you love.

In fact, if you plumb the depths of any one of these elements, you will find that the others will come to you of their own accord. For example, Albert Schweitzer chose his work on the basis of humanitarian service. Yet running through his work are the elements of integrity, joy, and excellence. On the other hand, Schweitzer's musical idol, Johann Sebastian Bach, chose his work on the basis of his joy, which is to say, his talent. Yet in his work we find great integrity and excellence, and centuries later, people are still served—uplifted and inspired—by it.

Each of these elements has its own call to the work you love: Integrity, the call of conscience; Service, the call of compassion; Enjoyment, the call of your talents; and Excellence, the call to greatness, the call of your destiny. The *conscience*, or inner voice, speaks to us through creative inspirations, visions, and intuitions. *Compassion* calls us to give our gifts, to do what we can to make the world a better place. *Talent* calls us to be the unique individuals that we are, to realize ourselves by expressing our innate abilities and developing our creative powers. *Destiny* calls us to realize that we were born to do something in this life—that we each have a role to play in the unfolding human drama.

Chapter 4

Integrity: The Call of Conscience

If I am not I, who will be?   —THOREAU

The first principle of integrity is: Be true to yourself. As Shakespeare said, "This above all,—to thine own self be true;/And it must follow, as the night the day,/Thou canst not then be false to any man." This is not only good moral advice, but a practical necessity of the creative life. For when you are separated from your "own self" (the voice of your conscience), you are left without the power of creative action.

Virtue is a word that means both "effective force or power" and "moral excellence." It is moral excellence, obedience to your own conscience, that gives you the effective force or power of creative action. Your conscience may from time to time tell you things you don't like hearing about yourself; but if you make a habit of ignoring it or turn it off altogether, you abandon the guiding force of your life and lose the power of creative action. Compromise your conscience and the power deserts you. Adhere to it once again and the power returns.

Your conscience, that still small voice deep within, is but an echo of the eternal and all-pervading intelligence of the universe. Listening to it gives you the sense that all is right with the world, that you are going with the flow of the universe, at one with its creative powers. Emerson said, "One who has access to this universal mind is party to all that is or can be done." From the standpoint of the individual ego, this universal creative mind has a mind of its own. It cannot be controlled or reasoned with; it must be followed. As Charlotte Brontë wrote, "[One] who possesses the creative gift owns something of which he is not always master—something that at times strangely wills and works for itself." What separates creative individuals from the rest is not so much their special talents or abilities but their capacity to hear and respond to this creative intelligence.

{It is} when I am, as it were, completely myself, entirely alone, and of good cheer . . . that ideas flow best and most abundantly. Whence and how they come, I know not, nor can I force them.

—MOZART

When some people hear the word *integrity*, they think of stodgy adherence to some abstract code of moral convention. We use the word in its original sense of "wholeness." The integrity of the creative life is not a matter of dutifully following all the rules and conventions of society, but of living as a whole person, integrated in mind, body, spirit, and emotions. With the voice of conscience as our center, all the elements of our being are in harmony. When we lose the center, the parts scatter and begin to war with one another.

Creative Integrity and the Inner Child

In youthful idealism man perceives the truth. In youthful idealism he possesses riches that should not be bartered for anything on earth.
— ALBERT SCHWEITZER

The creative individual is one who has successfully integrated the playful inner child with the capable, responsible adult. She is in touch with her childlike nature. One of the great keys to discovering the work you love is to ask the simple question, What did I want to give to the world when I was young and fresh, innocent and filled with wonder? Some of you will be able to recall right away. Others will first have to peel away the layers of hurt and defense that block your remembrance. You will first have to reintegrate your inner child.

When you were a child, you saw things simply. Your world was full of magic, wonder, and promise. The possibilities seemed limitless. You wanted to give your love and live in beauty, joy, and simplicity. You felt you could do or be anything. Perhaps grown-ups couldn't understand this world of yours, a world of endless whys, a world of magic and possibilities, a world that had yet to hear the word *compromise*.

Though perhaps not in so many words, you were told to compromise: compromise your dreams, compromise your ideals, compromise your sense of what's right for what would help you get along. Give in to the nothingness, the emptiness. Give in to becoming hollow and phony, a shell of a man, a mask of a woman. Hold up your masks, a different one for every scene. Show them what they want to see. But who is this actor? Has she no real life? Has he no story of his own? Where is integrity and joy in a masquerade life?

James Allen said, "The dreamers are the saviors of the world." Don't be afraid to admit that you have dreams, not only for yourself, but for your world. Don't be afraid to wonder and dream even as a child. This is not regression, but the height of genuine maturity. As Aldous Huxley wrote, "A child-like adult is not one whose development is arrested; on the contrary, he is an adult who has given himself a chance of continuing to develop long after most people have muffled themselves into a cocoon of middle age habit and convention." Most of us have grown old before our time. In our mental decrepitude, we have lost the ability to dream; we have gone blind to the possibilities. Our imaginations have shriveled and our worlds with them.

Throw off the disappointments, resentments, and

grudges that age you, and regain the vigor of creative youth. Determine to recover the creative vitality and natural enthusiasm for life that you knew as a child. Genius is, as Charles Baudelaire put it, "nothing more or less than childhood recovered by will, a childhood now equipped for self-expression with an adult's capacities." Truly, unless you become as a little child, you will never enter into the heavenly realm of creative living.

George Bernard Shaw said, "You see things and say, 'why?' but I dream things that never were and I say, 'why not?'" It was this attitude of mind that allowed Shaw to maintain a youthful vigor and playfulness into his nineties. While most a third his age had already grown old and dull, his childlike nature kept him not only young in spirit but creatively productive. As the Chinese philosopher Mencius said, "The great man is one who does not lose his childlike nature."

In your childhood, you could dream. Return. Let yourself return and simply imagine a world that works for everyone, a world of peace and justice, of freedom and brotherhood. Imagine a world where a child's desire to give is met not with indifference, doubt, or scorn but with praise, encouragement, and direction. Imagine a world where right is more important than might . . . a world where leaders become so because of their courage, integrity, and compassion . . . a world of beauty, where love is freely expressed and everyone works to give their best. Can you imagine it?

Now imagine what you can do about it. In claiming your vision for the world, you give yourself the gift of your best self, the one you always wanted to be, the one you knew you could be when you were a child, when you still believed in your possibilities. As you focus on that vision, the particular part for you to play in creating it will begin to come into view.

Youth is a quality, and if you have it, you never lose it.
—FRANK LLOYD WRIGHT

You can recover the energy and vitality of the inner child by getting in touch with things you loved to do as a child. Carl Jung recognized this dynamic psychological principle and used it to great effect in his own life. During a deep inner crisis following his break with Freud, he returned to his boyhood passion of building and constructing things. By putting himself in touch with his inner child, he found again his inspiration, exuberance, and passion for life. Reconnecting with the inner child helped him to find his own individual way in the world.

Learn again how to play, even as a child. One in touch with the vitality of the inner child throws himself into life. He is free to move spontaneously from intuition. His actions are neither dependent on the validation of others nor blocked by his own self-censure. No longer a mere observer or spectator, he actively participates in his life. This child-

73

like spirit of engagement is the road to life's work. As Thomas Merton said, "A man knows he has found his vocation when he stops thinking about how to live and begins to live."

Focusing Questions

- As a child, what did you most want to give to the world?
- As a child, what situation in the world most hurt, disturbed, or upset you? What did you want to do about it?
- When you were a child, what did you most love to do?
- If you could wave a magic wand and the world would instantly be the way you want it to be, how would it be different?

Creative Integrity and the Wisdom of Age

Live as you will have wished to have lived when you are dying.
—Christian Gellert

The Roman philosopher Cicero said, "I admire a young man who has something of the old man in him . . . [even as] I admire an old one who has something of a young man." The creative soul is one who has integrated not only the spirit and wonder of the child but the maturity and wisdom of age. When we lose touch with the inner child, we lose our sense of wonder, our natural exuberance for life. When we lose touch with the ancient one (the old man or woman within), we lose our sense of perspective.

One in touch with the wisdom of age realizes, even in her youth, that she will die, that her time upon this earth is but a brief season. Keeping her end in front of her, she is able to detach from the immediate rush of events and choose wisely how to spend her days. She lives not simply as a passive product of her culture, vacuously parroting its conventions and prejudices. Rather, by consciously choosing her own values and goals, she *creates* her culture and her world.

One of the great lessons of poetry, religion, and philosophy is this: Live in the awareness of death. Again, what seems like good moral advice is a key to creative empowerment and a means of tapping into the work you love. The key is learning to look from back to front. Mentally project yourself forward to the result you want to create; see it as complete or accomplished, and then identify the steps necessary to reach this outcome. This process works whether we want to create an object, an event, a business, or a life. It is one of the great secrets of creative living. To discover your life's work, or at least the values that you want to shape it, project yourself ahead to the end of your life and consider from this perspective what is and is not important. Ask yourself, When all is said and done, what do I want my life to have been about?

Any technique which will increase self-knowledge in depth should in principle increase one's creativity. —ABRAHAM MASLOW

In my youth, I spent a portion of my spare time visiting the elderly in nursing homes. I was struck, time and again, by how many of these people expressed regret about things they had always wanted to do with their lives, but hadn't. It wasn't just that they had failed to achieve their dreams: they had never even worked at them. Many had secretly cherished an idea of something they wanted to do for twenty or thirty years or more, but had never taken even the first step. On the other hand, there were a relative few who had lived their dreams and followed their heart's desire. They had an energy, a vitality, and a sense of humor that the others lacked. Moreover, they seemed more at peace with themselves and with the prospect of death. As one man told me, when I asked him if he feared dying, "Death is not a problem if you have lived first." Yet this man, and the few like him, were rare exceptions, bright spots in a sea of despair.

May you live all the days of your life. —JONATHAN SWIFT

The prevailing atmosphere of the nursing homes I visited was one of profound sadness and regret. It was poignant to hear these people—many bedridden, some with trembling hands—tell their stories of regret. Even more moving was the emphatic way they urged me, with all the strength and force they could muster, to follow my own dreams, not to allow what had happened to them to happen to me. Had this occurred once or twice, it would have made a strong impression, but its repetition left an indelible mark. I learned more about how to live from these people than from all the books I had ever read or classes I had ever taken. At that point, I determined not only to follow my own dreams but to dedicate my life to helping others, in whatever way I could, to avoid the fate that had befallen these poor souls.

When we realize what a frail and passing thing life is, our values come into sharp focus. In the awareness of the inevitability of death, it is easy to distinguish between what is truly important and what is of little moment. Over the years, in my consulting practice, I have worked with a number of people who were made suddenly and abruptly aware of their mortality. Some had been diagnosed with life-threatening illnesses; others had suffered the loss of a mate, close friend, or relative; a few had survived near-tragic accidents. These experiences jolted them out of their everyday routines and woke them up to the fact that they only had so much time on this earth. Their experiences sharpened their minds and made them determined to make the most out of their remaining years. Having committed themselves to restructuring their lives around what was really important to them, they were determined to find

77

careers that would express their real values and sense of purpose.

You needn't have such a dramatic experience to realize that your life, too, will end—that life itself is a precious gift, not to be squandered. Putting things off until someday is a bad habit and one we do well to break sooner rather than later. For days turn to months, and months to years, and before we know it, the future is here. As Horace said, "Those who postpone the hour of living as they ought are like the fool who waits for the river to pass before crossing; the river glides, and will forever." The best course is to seize this day, for you never know how many more you will have.

Focusing Questions

- Imagine that you've been told you have five years left to live. In terms of your work life, what is it that you most want to accomplish in your remaining years?
- Imagine yourself on your deathbed, filled with regret, with a painful sense of having missed your life's calling. What is it that you most regret not accomplishing?
- Now again, imagine yourself on your deathbed. This time, imagine that you feel at peace with the world and ready to pass on. You are surrounded by your friends and family. You feel as though you have completed or accomplished what you have come here to do in this life. What do you

consider to have been your most important accomplishments?

- More than anything, what do you want the message of your life to have been when all is said and done? How could you best exemplify this?

Creative Integrity and the Voice of Intuition

The greatest achievement was at first and for a time {only} a dream.
—JAMES ALLEN

One reason that we are not in touch with what we would love to do is that we have learned to censor ourselves and ignore our creative inspirations. A story about a young journalist will help to illustrate the stages we go through in the process of learning to censor our creative ideas. This young, idealistic journalist had visions of transforming the world through his crusading articles. One day, he got an idea for a story, which he wrote with great passion and excitement and eagerly submitted to his editor. The editor read the article and complimented the young journalist on the story, but told him that it was not really appropriate for publication. The next time the journalist got an idea for a crusading story, he didn't actually write it, but went to tell the editor about his idea. Again, the editor shot him down. The third time, he got an idea, but told *himself* that it wouldn't work. Finally, ideas for these kinds of stories no longer even occurred to him. Without realizing it, he internalized the groupthink of his profession as his own standard.

In the same way, many of us have learned to censor our own creative ideas. For us, the part of the editor may have been played by a parent, teacher, or guidance counselor. It may have been played by our friends or co-workers, by the media or popular culture. One way or another, we have had our dreams shot down, often while they were still in the germinal stage. This was experienced as painful or embarrassing and had a dampening effect on our creativity. Remembering this pain, we may have begun to label our creative inspirations as "silly" or "stupid," as "impractical" or "absurd," before anyone else could. We may have learned to dismiss our creative inspirations out of hand or even to suppress awareness of them altogether.

Much of the process of finding the work you love is a matter of learning to trust yourself once again, unlearning the habits of self-censorship. Give yourself the freedom to explore without the fear of looking foolish. Value your inspirations, even when they are still half-baked. As Linus Pauling, a two-time recipient of the Nobel Prize, put it, "You can't have a good idea without having a lot of ideas."

We cannot be creative and defensive at the same time. We must learn to lighten up on ourselves, to give our minds the freedom to explore and our hearts the freedom to be heard without being immediately subjected to criticism or analysis. It should be remembered that the greatest breakthroughs in any field appear at first to be irrational and absurd; for by definition, they do not fit the conventional way of viewing things.

Over the years, you may have had a number of inspirations or creative visions that you discounted as unrealistic or impractical. Reclaim these visions and you reconnect yourself with a powerful source of energy and inspiration. This is an essential part of being true to yourself. After all, your inspirations are not my inspirations or those of your friends or neighbors; they are uniquely your own. Learn to trust that inner voice that is trying to tell you what to do and how to live. As Mahatma Gandhi said, "Don't listen to friends when the Friend inside you says, 'Do this.'"

Following your own inspirations may require that, at times, you believe in the impossible—or at least in what seems impossible. For example, you might have seen yourself working in a field in which you currently have no background or training. You might have envisioned yourself working for some cause and yet see no way in which you could possibly make a living doing so. You might have had visions of starting a nonprofit organization or business and have no idea where to begin. You may have had an inspiration to buy a piano, though you have never had a lesson in your life. Don't dismiss your inspirations out of hand. Find the courage to say, with Albert Michaelson, "My greatest challenge is to attempt the impossible."

Focusing Questions

- Make a list of any and all inspirations you have had over the years that you haven't acted on or that you have given up on too easily.
- Look over your list and choose the three that are the most meaningful to you. List these in order of priority.
- Now select the one that speaks most powerfully to you and list a number of specific, active steps you could begin taking immediately toward turning this inspiration into reality.

Chapter 5

Service: The Call of Compassion

An individual has not started living until he can rise above the narrow confines of individualistic concerns to the broader concerns of all humanity. —MARTIN LUTHER KING, JR.

A pervasive sense of meaninglessness and alienation hangs over our modern civilization like a great dark cloud. The question of what to do about this sense of meaninglessness, alienation, or ennui, has been one of the great themes for writers, thinkers, and theologicans during the nineteenth and twentieth centuries. While it remains the subject of much erudite discussion and debate, there is a simple remedy to this great problem. As John Gardner put it, "When people are serving, life is no longer meaningless."

Meaningfulness begins with recognizing that you are not alone, that you are a part of the human community, that everything you do sends a ripple through the entire human family. Here then, lies another great key to discovering your life's work: Feel yourself a part of the great family of humankind and allow your natural compassion to suggest creative ways that you can serve this family of yours. Ask yourself, How is this, my human family, suffering? and To what is this, my human family, aspiring? Find a need that is going unmet and determine to fill it; find a desire for a fuller and richer experience of life and serve it. In so doing, you open a window to your own life purpose, your particular part in spreading joy or alleviating suffering in this world.

Dedicate your life to serving the aspirations and alleviating the sufferings of humankind, and you will have the sustained motivation necessary to develop your creative potential. You will discover what you are truly capable of. As the ancient philosopher Patanjali put it: "When you are inspired by some great purpose, some extraordinary project, all your thoughts break their bounds: Your mind transcends limitations, your consciousness expands in every direction, and you find yourself in a new, great and wonderful world. Dormant forces, faculties and talents become alive, and you discover yourself to be a greater person by far than you ever dreamed yourself to be."

As we discussed in chapter 1, the dichotomy between individual self-expression and meaningful service to others is a false one. We make this mistake only when we view self-expression in terms of consumption and acquisition—the silly notion that we express our individuality through the cars we drive or the clothes we wear, rather than through the release of our creative potential. Meaning is not to be found in acquisition, but in feeling ourselves a part of something greater. We cannot say it better than Tolstoy: "The sole meaning of life is to serve humanity."

84

Focusing Questions

- What problems in your world, nation, and community cry out most powerfully to you as needing action?
- What elements of human suffering speak to your heart?
- What human aspirations do you want most to champion or support?

Compassion: A Creative Response

I am never weary of being useful. . . . In serving others I cannot do enough. No labor is sufficient to tire me.

—LEONARDO DA VINCI

Walt Whitman said, "All music is what awakes within you when you are reminded of it by the instruments." Your life's work, the work you love, is what awakens within you when you are reminded of it by your compassion, your desire to give. It will not come to you by focusing on a desire to be better than others, by thinking about how you will survive, or by wishing everything in life were easy. It will come when you hear the call of your innate compassion for all of humankind.

The word *compassion* means literally "suffering with." Suffering is a part of life we cannot escape. We can, however, choose whether our suffering will be meaningful or pointless. Again, the difference comes down to who we think we are. We have been told that we are "by nature" self-interested creatures, that self-preservation is the compelling motivation behind human action. This belief is basic to our political and economic theories; it permeates popular culture. Yet it is one we do well to challenge. If self-preservation is all that drives us, how can we explain acts of heroism or self-sacrifice? How do we explain the individual who, at the risk of his or her own life, acts to save another? Indeed, who among us has not, at one time or another, acted for the benefit of another in the full knowledge that in so doing, we were bringing greater difficulties upon ourselves?

Self-preservation, the mere instinct to survive, we have in common with the animals. It is our compassion that makes us human. When we lose our compassion, our natural impulse to respond to the sufferings and aspirations of others, we have lost our humanity. We have, in some measure, become dead to the world. Truly, as Thoreau said, "The tragedy of a man's life is what dies inside of him while he lives." There is no greater tragedy than the death of compassion and no greater triumph than its rebirth.

As we die in selfishness, we live and grow in love. When we are obsessed with the concerns of our individual egos, we shrink our awareness; we feel small and petty. In compassion, we expand; we embrace a concept and experience of self beyond that of the separative ego. We become, as it were, "bigger" people. As Joseph Campbell put it, "When we quit thinking primarily about ourselves and our own self-preservation, we undergo a truly heroic transformation of consciousness." This transformation of consciousness, the birth of compassion, marks the beginning of a new, more vital and meaningful experience of life. From the perspective of this new life, the old ego-centered existence seems more like sleepwalking than living. This is what Martin Luther King, Jr., meant when he said that we only start to live when we "rise above the narrow confines of individualistic concerns to the broader concerns of all humanity."

Even if we wanted to, we could not separate ourselves from the rest of humanity or from anything else in the universe. Scientists tell us that we are star dust, that the very minerals that comprise our bodies and our world were generated by the explosions of stars in distant time and space. They tell us that every year, nearly all of the many billions of atoms that make up the human body are replaced. The atoms which today seem to belong to my nose may tomorrow find themselves in your kidneys or toes, or in a tree or a rose. Truly, as Walt Whitman said, "Every atom belonging to me as good belongs to you."

While we tend to think of our bodies as separate and solid, quantum mechanics tells us that they are in constant change, a part of a unified and fluid field of dynamic energy. Hippocrates, the "father" of Western medicine, long ago understood the spiritual implications of what it means to be a part of what he called, this "one common flow, one common breathing." It means, as he put it, *"All things are in sympathy."* To know what we truly are, then, is to be in sympathy with all things.

Compassion: A Question of Identity

The way to be happy is to make others so.
—ROBERT INGERSOLL

Compassion cannot be forced or faked, but flows naturally and spontaneously from the realization of identity. When we identify with others, we give freely and without reservation, for we give to ourselves. In the experience of identity, there is no condescension, self-righteousness, or arrogance. When we try to give without identity, it's a separate "me" doing "you" a favor, or a separate "us" helping "those people" who are all messed up. Compassion is not about trying to "do good" for those you feel separate from. It is the natural result of realizing that, in a fundamental and important way, you *are* the other.

Some may object that only a saint can love (identify with) everyone—and that may well be so—but we can all respond with compassion to those with whom we feel a special sense of identity, and in so doing, find meaning in our lives. When considering the work you are called to do, use this principle of sympathy in identity as a guide. Ask yourself: With whom or what do I especially identify? or, For whom or what do I feel a special sympathy or compassion?

For example, you may identify with neglected or abused children and determine to dedicate your life to serving them. Perhaps you identify with the psychological or physical pain of others and determine to become a psychologist, a medical doctor, or an alternative health practitioner. Perhaps you identify with victims of war or disaster and determine to make a life's work out of serving refugees. Perhaps you identify with those who suffer legal or political injustice and determine to become a lawyer or social activist. Perhaps you identify with immigrants who speak their new language with difficulty or embarrassment and determine to become a language teacher or tutor. You might identify with plants or animals and determine to become an ecologist or botanist, a veterinarian or zoologist.

Focusing Questions

- With whose aspirations or suffering do you especially identify?
- What situation or need in your community or world most rouses your sympathy?
- What do you want to do for these people or situations?

For Whom Are You Working?

So far we have discussed two ways in which creative compassion can lead you to your life's work: (1) to feel yourself a part of the entire human family and to ask, How is this family suffering? and To what is it aspiring? (2) to become aware of those individuals, groups, or causes with which you feel a special identity and compassion. As well as considering whom you want to serve, give some consideration to the scope of the impact you want to make. Is the change you want to make or the contribution you want to offer at the level of the individual, the community, the nation, or the world? How many lives do you want to reach, and at what level or depth?

The most sublime act is to set another before you.
—WILLIAM BLAKE

Some are called to serve the multitudes, some to minister to a select few. Discover what is best for you. Either can be a great work. For, finally, service is not a matter of numbers, but of love. We cannot love even one person—deeply and completely—without discovering that, in the process, we have learned to love everyone.

Focusing Questions

- How do you work best: alone, one on one, in small groups, or within large organizations?
- What scale would you like to work on: local, national, or international?

Compassion: The Key to Purpose

This is the true joy in life, the being used for a purpose recognized by yourself as a mighty one. —GEORGE BERNARD SHAW

In this cynical age we live in, the idea of having a purpose in life is considered by some to be nothing more than a superstitious holdover from the prescientific past. They will tell you that human beings are the result of random genetic mutations, that all we are and all we do is just so much biochemistry. They will tell you that purpose is a relic, a fiction trumped up by religion in the dark ages of the past. Yet you don't have to be religious to believe that you're here for a reason, that there is a purpose for your existence. You have only to consider the alternative. What if your life has no purpose? Are we to believe that we are just so many ants rushing to and fro until it is our time to go?

Even if we believe that life itself is an accident, we cannot deny that we are all in this thing together, nor can we deny that what we do or don't do has a profound effect, not only on our fellow beings, but on all the world. Human beings have the power to think and to create. For better or for worse, we dream, we imagine, and we shape our world in the image of our dreams. We cannot do otherwise. By the dreams we choose, we are deciding whether our children will live in a hellish or beautiful world. No, you needn't be religious to believe that you are here for a reason; you have only to consider the alternative. As Edmund Burke put it, "The only thing that is necessary for the triumph of evil is for the good men [and women] to do nothing."

Your purpose is your particular response to the needs and aspirations of humankind. The things of the world you find most troubling, painful, or upsetting, the aspirations and longings of your fellow beings—these are powerful keys to the discovery of your life's work. You might work against poverty, injustice, indignity, ill health, or mental deprivation. Martin Luther King, Jr., and Mahatma Gandhi were moved by the lack of dignity and justice with which human beings treated each other. You might work for beauty and truth, joy and understanding. Einstein was touched by a desire to understand the mysteries of the universe. Mozart was moved to write music that still inspires us today. Luther Burbank was moved to discover how plants and man could better care for one another. Whether you are working to end suffering or to spread joy, you play a part in building the world you want to live in. Whether you discover your purpose in a flash of inspiration or after long and careful reflection, go with what moves you the most.

To have a great purpose to work for, a purpose larger than ourselves, is one of the secrets of making life significant, for then the meaning and worth of the individual overflow his personal borders and survive his death. —WILL DURANT

Finding the work you love is not a cerebral process. It is not a matter of figuring something out through a process of rational analysis. It is a process of opening yourself and beginning to pay attention to what you respond to with energy and enthusiasm. Pay attention to the people, events, and activities in the outside world that evoke the strongest response from you. Pay attention as well to your inside world, to the inspirations and intuitions that most excite you. From within and without, let yourself be moved. Listen to your own heart and learn to trust what it is saying.

While your heart *knows,* your head can only suppose. It is in the nature of the conscious rational mind to doubt. We never decide with certainty when we decide with our heads, for there are always at least two sides to every argument. With our heads we think, Perhaps this is the right path; but then we begin to doubt, thinking, Oh, but what about this other way? You can only fully commit yourself to and invest yourself in your work when you *know* that you are on the right course, and it is precisely this total commitment that, more than anything else, will determine your success.

While your head cannot be trusted to make important life decisions, it can be extremely useful in executing them. Use your head to chart the course inspired by your heart. Let your head and heart work together. Just make sure that your head knows who is boss. After all, since what you are looking for is the work you love, it is surely your heart that holds the key. And nothing opens the door to your heart like compassion.

Listen to your conscience, respond to your natural compassion, and you will never be troubled by feelings of meaninglessness or alienation. We *are* social beings. In big ways and in small, we touch the lives of all we come in contact with. Nothing is more satisfying than knowing you are making a constructive difference in the lives of others. As the modern philosopher J. Krishnamurti put it, "It is more important to find out what you are giving to society than to ask what is the right means of livelihood." It is more important to find out what you are giving to the world than to ask, What is the right career or job for me? "Finding what you want to give to the world" is another way of saying "finding your purpose in life" or "finding the work you love."

You *are* here for a reason. Determine to discover it! Look

within your heart and out upon the world. Look at how much the world needs your love and how much you want to give it. Then determine to live your life on purpose, with a purpose you recognize as a mighty one.

Focusing Question

- What is the purpose of your life? What is your part to play in making the world a better place?

Chapter 6

Enjoyment: The Call of Talent

Everyone has a vocation, talent is the call. — EMERSON

As much as integrity to conscience and service to others, joy is an absolute requirement of a life's work. Man was not made for drudgery or tedium. Life is a thing to be tasted, celebrated, and enjoyed. The great joy in work is in self-expression, following the way of your natural talents. Through the voice of conscience, we hear the echo of the intelligence that, as Heraclitus put it, "steers all the universe." In compassion, we respond tò the sufferings and aspirations of others. By developing our unique talents, we realize the joys of individual self-expression.

Talent, then, is another great key to finding the work you love. Talent is a vehicle for the discovery of your life's work, both in its own right, and as a means of giving shape and form to the inspirations of conscience and the calls of compassion. Where conscience or compassion is the seed of a life's work, talent is the soil in which it grows. Two people may have an identical vision or purpose, yet each finds a way to express it that is uniquely his or her own. Each expresses it according to his or her unique talents and abilities.

Talent: The Joy of Doing What Comes Naturally

If you do what you like, you never really work. Your work is your play.
*—*HANS SEYLE

Your talents are revealed in the things that come naturally to you. Some things are natural to all of us as human beings. Because we are human, we breathe, eat, sleep, and excrete; we sit, stand, walk, talk, and so on. We didn't choose any of these things, any more than we chose to have two eyes instead of one or three. In the same way, your talents are those things that come naturally to you as an individual. Talents are not chosen, but recognized. They cannot be learned, but they can and should be developed. Don't confuse your special innate talents with the many skills you may have learned over the years. When looking for the work you love, talent is a much better indicator than skill. Awareness of your skills comes into play when executing the work you love, while knowledge of your talents is crucial to its initial discovery.

To know your talents is to know your strengths, and this knowledge is vital to your happiness. As Jonathan Swift wrote: "Although men are accused of not knowing their own weakness, yet perhaps few know their strength. It is in men as in soils, where sometimes there is a vein of gold which the owner knows not of." To go through life without ever knowing or expressing your talents is the worst form of poverty and self-denial.

Expressing our talents feels so good because we enjoy doing what we are naturally good at. We feel pleasure in expressing ourselves and experience pain when our natural self-expression is somehow blocked. People who have never known the pleasure of expressing their own unique talents often associate work with pain and struggle or, at best, think of it as a duty that must be performed in order to achieve some benefit or result. They have never known the joy of working for its own sake.

Many people feel as though they must check certain parts of themselves at the office or factory door—that in order to fit into their job slots or positions, they must shave off important aspects of themselves. Perhaps it is their energy, leadership ability, or compassion; perhaps it their humor, intelligence, or initiative that they must check at the door. The old adage "use it or lose it" definitely applies to our talents. After many years of working without expressing them, we may begin to feel that we have hardly anything left to check. We may come to believe that what we are doing is all that we will ever be capable of doing. We may begin to doubt that we have any special gifts or abilities at all.

The Chinese have a saying: "The duck's legs are short, but if we try to lengthen them, the duck will feel pain. A crane's legs are long, but if we try to cut off a portion of them, the crane will feel grief. We are not to amputate what is by nature long, or to lengthen what is by nature short." Too many people feel the pain and grief, the self-loathing and resentment, that result from denying their own natures and spending their lives trying to be something they are not. Such people are likely to feel defeated and overwhelmed, for they are going through their lives with their hands tied behind their backs. But show me a man or woman who uses his or her God-given talents to the utmost, and I will show you a person brimming with inner confidence.

William Du Bois wrote: "The return from your work must be the satisfaction which that work brings you and the world's need of that work. With this, life is heaven, or as near heaven as you can get. Without this—with work which you despise, which bores you, and which the world does not need—this life is hell." We can only find satisfaction in the work itself when we are expressing ourselves through it. We all desire to make a difference in this life, and since your talents are your greatest strengths, it is through their expression that you will have the greatest impact on the world around you. This is a joy you don't want to miss.

Blessed is he who has found his work. Let him ask no other blessing. —THOMAS CARLYLE

As we have said, bottled-up creative energy is a great source of stress in life. It is energy that wants to move and find expression. When it is not released into the outer world, it builds up within, generating anxiety and restlessness. We cannot know inner peace until we develop our own channels for creative release. As Abraham Maslow put it, "A musician must make his music, an artist must paint, a poet must write if he is to ultimately be at peace with himself."

Focusing Questions

- What do you most enjoy doing?
- What do you most enjoy thinking about?
- What do you most enjoy learning about?
- Over all, what do you feel are your strongest talents?

If you fail to express your talents, you will cause yourself all of the pains and miss out on all of the joys listed below.

The Pains of Repressing Your Talents

- *The Pain of Self-Denial:* It hurts to deny yourself and to try to be and do something that is not really you.
- *The Pain of Limitation:* It hurts to—day after day—do work not really suited to your talents.
- *The Pain of Meaninglessness:* It hurts to know that you could be doing far more than you are.
- *The Pain of Stagnation:* It hurts to block the flow of creative energy.
- *The Pain of Boredom:* It hurts to feel trapped in the confines of ego and the pressures of time.

The Pleasures of Expressing Your Talents

- *The Joy of Your Nature:* It feels good to do what is really you.
- *The Joy of Strength:* It feels good to do what you are naturally good at.
- *The Joy of Feedback:* It feels good to see yourself making your strongest impact.
- *The Joy of Energy Flow:* It feels good to let creative energy move through you.
- *The Joy of Self-Forgetting:* It feels good to become absorbed, to lose yourself in your work.

Talent: The Place to Find and Lose Yourself

Whosoever shall seek to save his life shall lose it; and whosoever shall lose his life shall preserve it. —LUKE 17:33

In the expression of your talents, you both find and lose yourself. By recognizing and developing your special talents and abilities, you come to know yourself as a unique individual. Through the whole of nature we hear the cry, Be yourself! Be yourself! The lark does not sing the song of the nightingale, nor does the apple tree become ripe with cherries. Though we humans tend to complicate things with self-conscious thoughts, it is in truth no different for us.

The Chinese have a saying: "If by nature a man is a strong man, he will carry a very heavy burden without feeling the weight. If one is by nature a skillful man, he can manage all sorts of affairs without feeling busy." So it is for all of us. If we do what we are naturally good at, we find the way of life easy. Find your way by recognizing and appreciating your talents. Trust that you were born with special gifts and work to discover and realize these. Say to yourself, as Walt Whitman said to himself, "Walt, you contain enough, why don't you let it out then?"

Be and express what you are by nature and you may begin to transcend nature itself—opening a window on the infinite. As Carl Jung put it, "In knowing ourselves to be unique, we possess the capacity for becoming conscious of the infinite. But only then!" This is one of the great paradoxes of life: the way to transcend nature is to honor it. Be what you are, and you discover that you are more than you thought.

Every religion teaches that we must lose ourselves to find ourselves. Again, what seems like good moral advice is a great key to creative living. Self-forgetfulness was traditionally held to be a fundamental goal, not only of religion, but of art. Within traditional cultures, art was not limited to what we today call the fine arts, but encompassed all manner of doing and making. As one noted art historian put it, "The artist was not a special kind of person, but each person a special kind of artist." All were encouraged to approach their work as an art, and in so doing, to enter into the joy of self-forgetfulness. This is the natural high or orgasm of work. The joy of the sexual orgasm is the temporary self-extinction that occurs when pleasure becomes so unbearably intense that the self-conscious mind must give way.

The self-forgetfulness of creative engagement occurs when the individual becomes so absorbed in her work that she loses all self-consciousness and merges with, or becomes one with, the work itself. As Riciotto Canudo put it, "It is certain that the secret of all art . . . lies in self-oblivion." The modern sculptor Antoine Bourdelle said, "The secret of art is love." These two "secrets" are really one and the same. We can only know the joys of self-forgetting by doing work we truly love. For to achieve the absorption necessary for self-forgetfulness requires great concentration, and we only reach this intensity of concentration when we love what we are doing.

Traditional religion, philosophy, and art theory understood the psychological problem of life to be one of self-liberation, of gaining freedom from the self. Fixation on the ego was held to be the source of our inner misery. Traditionally, work was viewed as a means of freeing ourselves from preoccupation with the ego, and thus as a path to self-liberation. On the other hand, modern psychology tells us that the psychological problem is one of self-correction and adaptation. The self is not to be forgotten but corrected. With few notable exceptions, modern psychology has had precious little to say about the role that creative expression in work plays in psychological health.

It seems that every day, psychologists are coming up with new "disorders" or "dysfunctions." They are constantly discovering new things which must be fixed or corrected before we can be happy. We can easily become overwhelmed with all that is wrong with us. Many people spend the whole of their lives trying to fix themselves, preparing for some day in the future when they will be ready to live. They think of themselves as damaged goods, incapable of fully living until they are fixed or repaired. In the end, playing Dr. Fix-it never works, for it never ends.

Again, we must ask the question, Who or what are we? Are we machines that must be constantly fixed and repaired? Or are we organic beings with an innate desire to express ourselves? If you spend your time learning to express in the present rather than endeavoring to fix your past, you will be much better off. As Emerson said, "A man is relieved and gay when he has put his heart into his work and done his best; what he has said or done otherwise shall give him no peace."

Life is meant to be expressed, not to be analyzed or fixed. You will never get to your strengths by focusing on your weaknesses. You grow in strength as you focus on and develop your strengths. If, instead of looking at all the ways in which you think you are broken, you concentrate on doing what you naturally do well, you will feel yourself grow in confidence and ability. The feeling of joy and aliveness that results is nature's way of telling you that you are on track.

Focusing Question

• What were you doing the last time that you were so absorbed that you lost all track of time?

Talent: Pleasure in the Making

When I work, I relax. Doing nothing . . . makes me tired.
— PABLO PICASSO

We have said that the great joy in work comes through the full expression of your talents. Yet if you have lost touch with your innate abilities, you may have to go on a journey of self-discovery to find them again. The road to the discovery and full expression of your talents goes by the way of attitude and creative resourcefulness. We can think of a scale of enjoyment in work beginning with attitude, moving into creative resourcefulness, and culminating with the expression of talent. A person with a negative attitude is not likely ever to develop their talents, nor is one who has made a habit of looking at all that is lacking or missing in her life.

Again, enjoyment is to be found in what comes naturally. We are naturally happy and positive in our feeling towards life and must learn to become bitter or negative. We are naturally creatively resourceful and must learn to hesitate and doubt our capacity to handle the opportunities and challenges which life presents. We naturally move toward our talents, for the expression of talents is pleasurable and we spontaneously move toward pleasure. We have to learn to associate self-expression with pain, and to become resigned to settling for less than happiness.

ENJOYMENT IS AN ATTITUDE

As soon as possible, begin doing work that you love and enjoy, work that allows you to take full advantage of your innate talents and abilities. In the meantime, don't allow a negative attitude to steal your joy and rob you of the energy that you will need to make the transition. It is certainly more pleasurable to come to work with joy and gratitude than with resentment and hostility. If all the while you're working, you're thinking to yourself, Oh, I hate doing this. Why am I here? Oh, this is so awful!— you are going to get bogged down and have little fun besides. But if you think, How can I have fun with what I am doing?—you increase your pleasure.

People are about as happy as they make up their minds to be.
—ABRAHAM LINCOLN

We add joy simply by embracing and not resisting what is in front of us to do, whether it's going to the office, raking leaves, or doing the dishes. Resist what resists in you, and let your natural enjoyment come through. This is a matter not only of enjoyment but of effectiveness. As Terence said, "There is nothing so easy but that it becomes difficult when you do it reluctantly."

Suffering is meaningful when it is endured in love for something larger than oneself. Suffering is necessary when it is rooted in the human condition. This is the suffering inherent in life itself, born from the fact that we reside in frail bodies that will expire in seventy to perhaps one hundred years. It is compounded by the fact that we live in a world plagued by sickness, wracked by violence, and burdened with terrible injustice, poverty, and ignorance.

This, it might seem, is suffering enough, and yet many heap on added misery through negativity and bitterness. This is the worst of all suffering. It is neither meaningful nor necessary, but a kind of self-inflicted torture. Truly, as Sophocles said, "The greatest griefs are the ones we cause ourselves." Don't let yourself become what George Bernard Shaw called "a feverish little clod of ailments and grievances complaining that the world will not devote itself to making you happy." This will only leave you feeling hopeless and depressed. On the other hand, enjoyment and appreciation of life energizes you and gives you confidence in the future.

Focusing Questions

- In what ways, if any, are you allowing negative thought patterns to cause you needless suffering and sap your creative energy? What has this cost you so far in terms of your life and your work?

• Realizing that happiness and enjoyment are, finally, the result of a decision, how could you bring enjoyment to things you have been resisting, avoiding, or denying?

ENJOYMENT IS A CREATIVE RESPONSE

The next level of enjoyment in work comes with developing the confidence to handle whatever may come your way. This is the confidence of creative resourcefulness. Human beings are by nature a resourceful lot. Our species has developed creative strategies for living in virtually any environment, from the thickest jungles to the highest mountain regions, from searing deserts to the most frigid regions of our planet. Consider the Eskimos. They didn't think, Well, there are no trees or stones here. We can't build a shelter; we will wait to die of exposure. They built shelters with what was at hand, out of snow. They didn't think, Oh, we can't grow food here, and there is little game; we will starve. They took advantage of, and wisely managed, the few food sources available.

Traditional peoples not only managed to take care of their material needs but found ways to express their spiritual and creative aspirations in all kinds of environments. The Paiutes lived in the region known as the Great Basin of the American West. These were desolate lands, incapable of supporting permanent settlement. The people wandered over vast stretches in small family bands. Constantly on the move and with few available resources, they nevertheless found ways to creatively express themselves. Indeed, they became the finest basket weavers the world has ever known. The Paiutes wove so skillfully, so tightly that they could carry water in grass baskets made without sealant. These baskets were not only highly functional; they were objects of incredible beauty. Again, human beings are by nature creative and highly resourceful. It is in our nature to take what is at hand and not only make it do, but do so beautifully.

Think not so much of what thou hast not, as of what thou hast.
—MARCUS AURELIUS

Humankind did not lose this innate creative resourcefulness simply because we began living in modern urban environments. Yet we have muddled our natural ability by learning to think that what is missing is more important than what is at hand. Too often we think, Oh, I would do it, but I don't have X, or If only I had Y, then I would do it. Your creativity is measured by what you do with what you have, not by what you might do if you had something you think you lack. *If you always go as far as you can with what you have, you will always find that you can always go further.* Ninety percent of developing your talent is simply developing the discipline to stop making excuses and get down to work. *And* the discipline to keep working at it every day. Developing creative resourcefulness is just a nice way of saying "get your rear in gear." As Seneca said, "Let him who would move the world first move himself."

Robert Johnson, the great blues guitarist of the 1920s, was a man with a passion and an innate talent for music that would not be denied. Unable to afford a guitar, he made one himself out of materials available to him as a tenant farmer. He couldn't pay for lessons and had no one to teach him, so he taught himself how to play. Johnson went on to develop a style of play that was to influence his field of music for many years to come. I once heard of a boy whose parents couldn't afford even to rent a piano. He taught himself how to read music and practiced by fingering pieces on a life-size drawing he made of the piano keys. If we could develop this kind of passion to express our talents, there is no telling what we could do. Again, you don't have to learn how to be resourceful; you have only to unlearn the thought processes that block your natural creativity. Resist the temptation to focus on what you lack and make the best use of what you have. If you know how to use it, you truly have everything you need.

Focusing Questions

- What, more than anything, do you feel is keeping you from creating a more fulfilling experience of work (e.g., a lack of time, money, training, education, connections, etc.)?
- What steps could you be taking right now to overcome these obstacles?

Talent: Love Opens the Door

To enjoy—to love a thing for its own sake and for no other reason.   —LEONARDO DA VINCI

The middle-eastern poet Rumi said, "Everyone has been made for some particular work, and the desire for that work has been put in his [or her] heart." Listen to your heart. It is there that you will be guided—by the voice of your conscience, by your creative compassion, and your desire for self-expression—to the fulfillment of your destiny. This gives another principle that leads to the discovery of a life's work: *Anything that helps you to get in touch with your heart will move you closer to your life's work.*

Many of us do not get a chance to do what we love in our work. Often in our relationships, we give up things we love because our partner doesn't enjoy or approve of them. Or we simply get into a routine and forget to do things that we really enjoy. After a while it can seem as though we aren't having any fun. Spend some time doing things you love to do. Put in a garden. Take a hike in the wilderness. Go to a concert or play. Take a walk on the beach. Spend a day in a park. Make a new friend. Listen to music you love. Have a conversation with an interesting person. Watch your favorite movies. Prepare your favorite meals. Have a party. Dance. Reread your favorite books or read one you have been meaning to get to. Take a trip. Organize a softball or volleyball game. Doing things you love to do will move you closer to your heart. It will help you to remember how much you can enjoy life. It will energize you and help you to believe again in the possibilities.

Focusing Questions

- What things do you most love to do? Make a list of at least a dozen. Schedule time to do as many as you can.
- Take another look at your list and ask yourself, Is there any way I might be able to make a living doing any of these things?

Chapter 7

Excellence: The Call to Greatness

In the long run you hit only what you aim at. Therefore, though you should fail immediately, you had better aim at something high.
— THOREAU

There is something within all of us that aspires to greatness, something that calls us to be the best we can be, to do the highest quality work we are capable of. While the content of your life's work will be determined by your inspirations, sense of purpose, and talents, the quality of your work will depend on your expectations of yourself. Even more to the point, your expectations will determine the size of your dreams. Since we never rise higher than our aspirations, in choosing your aspirations you are choosing your life. To allow yourself to settle for less than your best is to decide to spend your life hounded and haunted by the ghost of might-have-been. It is to fail your conscience, your fellow man, and your talents. It is to fail your destiny.

The commitment to excellence requires that we put aside any false modesty. It is not a sign of arrogance to expect great things of ourselves. Some people take great pride in their limitations, in how intractable and stubborn their personal problems are. If we are to have pride, let it be in our accomplishments, not in our limitations.

Greatness is the birthright of every human being, available to all who will claim it. As Martin Luther King, Jr., put it, "Everybody can be great. Because anybody can serve. You don't have to have a college degree to serve. You don't have to make your subject and verb agree to serve. You don't have to know about Plato and Aristotle . . . Einstein's Theory of Relativity . . . [or] the Second Theory of Thermodynamics in physics to serve. You only need a heart full of grace. A soul generated by love."

If we are all capable of greatness, how, then, do we go about realizing it? Shakespeare said, "Some are born great; some achieve greatness, and some have greatness thrust upon them." Great or not, we have already been born, equipped at birth with all our natural abilities and talents. We could wait to have greatness thrust upon us, but we might spend our lives waiting for a thrust that never comes. For most of us, then, if we are ever to know greatness, it will be by the remaining course. It will be because we have consciously and deliberately determined to achieve it. As William Jennings Bryan said, "Destiny is not a matter of chance, it is a matter of choice; it is not a thing to be waited for, it is a thing to be achieved."

Excellence: A Matter of Expectation

Hold yourself responsible for a higher standard than anyone else expects of you. Never excuse yourself.
— HENRY WARD BEECHER

Expectation is the *context* in which we hold the events of our lives. It's an intangible that sets one person apart from others. While we can't see the internal thought process of another, we can see its effects on his or her life. It's easy to spot those who expect a lot of themselves. Even in young people who have no track record to speak of, you can see it in their bearing and manner, in the way they do the little things. The sense of self-respect and belief in their destiny that they project gives them an aura of greatness. People who expect a lot of themselves are the ones you want on your team, whether you're playing basketball or business, whether you are looking for a marriage partner or a director for your nonprofit corporation.

Your talents indicate and, to a degree, limit what you *can* do. Your expectations determine what you *will* do. The whole effort of realizing the work you love is one of converting your "cans" into "wills." Expectation is the mental environment in which your talents will either be nurtured and developed or repressed and stunted. While you can no more change your innate talents than the color of your eyes, you can change your expectations.

Truly, we rise or fall with our expectations. Our expectations affect the way we view, approach, and do everything. Holding the expectation of greatness, having a sense of destiny about your life, is more important than having a crystal clear picture of the form your work will take. That will unfold as time goes along, and it may change.

We have repeatedly emphasized that to find anything, it helps to know what you are looking for. It also helps to expect that you will find it. Whether you are looking for a misplaced set of keys, a turn on a desolate, rural highway, or the work you love—expecting to find what you are looking for makes all the difference. It allows you to relax, stay focused on your objectives and moving toward them. It reduces the impatience and sense of frustration that might cause you to give up. While we all encounter difficulties and setbacks on the way to realizing our dreams, those who expect that they will ultimately succeed persist long after others have given up.

YOU GET WHAT YOU EXPECT—SO EXPECT THE BEST

Of course we want to realize our dreams and achieve our full potential, but when what we want conflicts with what we expect, we get what we expect, not what we want. Whether you expect yourself to do little, be "average," or make an outstanding contribution, expectation is the key to performance. Here, then, is another great key to finding and fulfilling your life's work: *Expect that you will. Believe in your destiny.*

Always bear in mind that your own resolution to succeed is more important than any other one thing. —ABRAHAM LINCOLN

If you study the lives of the so-called greats of history, you will see time and time again that these people had a sense of destiny about them. They believed that they would ultimately be successful. That belief sustained them through dark periods when, by all appearance, they had no right or reason to believe that they would prevail.

It is low expectations, more than any lack of talent, character flaw, or external barrier, that keep us from realizing our full potential. Have you ever looked at a friend, relative, or loved one and thought to yourself: If he could only see what I see. . . . He has so much potential. . . . If only he believed in himself. It may not occur to you that people might be looking at you and thinking: If only she believed in herself . . . oh, what she could do! While we can't change the expectations of others, we can change our own.

Perhaps there is no greater example of the power of expectations than creativity itself. Studies were conducted to discover if there are any identifiable environmental or genetic characteristics that could be linked to creativity.

Researchers looked at I.Q., social and economic background, education, and a number of other variables. The only variable that was found to in any way correlate with creativity, as measured by the researchers, was the individual's belief that he or she was creative. People who believe they are creative actually are more so. Even if you have doubts, claim your creativity and watch it grow.

UNDERSTANDING LOW EXPECTATIONS

As a psychology student, I, like all college freshmen, was required to participate in psychological experiments. In one such study, the object was to measure the effects of positive and negative reinforcement on performance. Subjects were divided into two groups and were asked to learn and perform a simple task. In one group, the individual assigned to execute the task was provided with a partner who was to continually offer encouraging statements such as "I know you can do it," "You are doing very well," and so on. In the other group, the partner was to continually harass the subject by telling them how stupid they were, how they would never get it, how poorly they were performing, and so on.

Selected to play the part of a harassing partner, I refused to participate in the experiment. The effect it was designed to demonstrate seemed obvious on its face and not worth terrorizing an unwitting victim for. (Researchers had instructed us to continue with the harassment even if the individual broke down and began to cry or became angry.) We certainly don't need studies to tell us that people learn and perform better in the face of encouragement and the expectation of success than they do under constant belittlement.

No one can make you feel inferior without your consent.
—ELEANOR ROOSEVELT

Yet, unfortunately, many of us carry around a harassing partner inside our own heads. It's constantly telling us that we will never amount to much, that we shouldn't risk disappointment by expecting too much of ourselves. Or it tells us that we are too stupid, too lazy, too undisciplined—too whatever—to expect that we will ever touch greatness. In the course of our upbringing, many of us became accustomed to settling for less, habituated to low expectations. Saddled with a negative self-image, we never got the idea that we could, should, or would accomplish anything great.

It is not difficult to understand why. In a research study conducted at Iowa University, graduate students followed two-year-olds around and recorded every time their parents said something positive to them and every time they said something negative. The results were startling. On average, the children heard fourteen negative statements for every positive one. This early indoctrination into negativity is internalized and carried over into later life.

A simple study conducted among college freshmen at UCLA demonstrates the pervasiveness of negative self-image. As one of the most prestigious universities in the California system, UCLA has relatively high admissions standards. Its college freshmen represent the "best and brightest" of their generation. Yet when these students were asked to list their strengths and weaknesses, their lists averaged six times more weaknesses than strengths. It is probably safe to say that *most* people are going through life carrying heavy burdens of negative beliefs that limit their expectations of and for themselves.

RAISING YOUR EXPECTATIONS: NURTURING YOUR MIND

If we could replace, once and for all, the inner voice of the harassing partner with that of an encouraging partner, we would see our capabilities soar. Fortunately, we can. Napoleon Hill, author of the classic success book *Think and Grow Rich*, grew up in abject poverty. He recognized that as a result of his upbringing, he had been programmed with a mindset of poverty. He knew that unless he deliberately intervened and changed his thought processes, his fate was sealed. Since he had already been conditioned to expect a life of poverty, he knew it was up to him to change his mind and give himself a higher standard to live up to. He understood that we cannot rise above our expectations.

Nurture your minds with great thoughts. To believe in the heroic makes heroes. —BENJAMIN DISRAELI

While we may not have grown up with the kind of poverty that Hill experienced, many of us are, in our own ways, limited by low expectations. For example, many expect that they will be materially comfortable, but don't expect to have much fun making their living. Others hold the belief that they can't both provide for themselves and serve others, that they must choose between doing something noble and doing something monetarily rewarding. Others expect that they will never have the opportunity to creatively express themselves in their work.

While our limiting beliefs are a result of our upbringing, it is futile to waste time wishing that we had been raised differently. The better course is to raise yourself to a new level of expectation. Your parents (or parental surrogates) raised you for the first eighteen years or so. Yet with a normal life span, you will have another sixty years to raise yourself. Don't waste time crying over spilt milk. Begin at once to fill your mind with all the encouragement, confidence, and high expectations you can muster. Imagine that you are again an innocent and trusting child. What would you want to tell this child? What expectations would you want to hold for his or her life? William James said, "Human beings can alter their lives by altering their attitudes of mind." Alter your expectations and you alter what is possible for you to achieve.

A man's dreams are an index to his greatness.
—ZADOK RABINOWITZ

Since he wanted to be successful, Napoleon Hill made a point of studying the principles, or what he called "laws," of success. He saturated his mind with the thoughts he knew would bring success. He realized that thoughts show no respect of person, that great people are great *because* they think great thoughts. Take a person with the greatest talent and potential in the world, let him think low and miserable thoughts, and he will not amount to much. Take another with a quarter of his potential, let her mind be saturated with great thoughts, and she will shake the world. As someone once said, "You are as important as what you think about all day." More than what we eat, we are what we think.

Hill employed another useful technique, which he referred to as the "master mind" principle. This technique involves creating a kind of peer group of the mind. By reading the writings, biographies, and letters of the greats of history, you begin to identify with them as people like yourself. You break down the artificial barrier between yourself and greatness. As you "make friends with" great people, you begin to engage them in mental conversation, seeking insight, advice, and direction. You start to think the kinds of thoughts they thought, to expect of yourself the kinds of things they expected of themselves. You make common cause with those who have endeavored to hold up the light of human possibilities in every arena of human experience. You develop a deep sense of gratitude for their efforts.

As you appreciate the efforts of those who have gone before, you develop a sense of responsibility to those who will come after. Albert Einstein put it like this: "Many times a day I realize how much my own inner and outer life is built on the labors of other men, both living and dead, and how earnestly I must exert myself in order to give in return as much as I have received." This sense of responsibility is an essential characteristic of individuals who achieve excellence in any field. As Michael Korda put it: "Success on any major scale requires you to accept responsibility. . . . In the final analysis, the one quality that all successful people have . . . is the ability to take on responsibility."

MAKING THE RIGHT KIND OF FRIENDS

While creating a mental peer group can be a powerful tool for raising our expectations, even more important is the company we keep in daily life. Emerson said, "The one thing we need is someone to make us do what we are capable of doing." Of course, no one can *make* or force us to do anything. Yet getting to know people who expect a lot of themselves can help us to realize that we, too, can do more than we once thought. Understanding how important expectations are will help us to choose our friends wisely, to gravitate toward those who will tend to lift us up and to avoid as intimates those we can't count on to believe in us. Be careful in the friends you select. Remember: like misery, self-pity, blame, and excuse love company. The best friend you can have is one who you know loves and accepts you and yet challenges you to be your best, one who isn't afraid to tell you the truth.

Tell me with whom you go & I'll tell you what you do.
　　　　　　　　　　—WILLIAM BLAKE

The terms "soft enemies" and "enablers" have been used to describe people who, while apparently supportive, actually encourage the low expectations that deprive us of happiness and success. While we tend to be wary of those who are openly hostile and negative toward our dreams, we are often lulled by those who give the outward appearance of supporting us by encouraging and coddling limited views of ourselves. Precisely because we tend to have our guards down around these people, they can have an even more devastating influence on our self-esteem than those who are openly hostile. Our soft enemies do not necessarily have any vicious or evil intent. In all likelihood, they are themselves unconscious of the subtle ways they put us down. Yet one way or another, they communicate that they don't really expect much of us. Remember that people can't believe in you any more than they believe in themselves. The only people who can consistently wish you happiness are those who are themselves consistently happy. The only ones who can inspire you to excellence are those who are themselves committed to it.

Many people have never known what it is like to have anyone who really believed in them. Consequently, they are often suspicious and have difficulty trusting others. Indeed, they may feel threatened when someone comes along and challenges them to consider whether or not they are expecting the best of themselves. They are likely to be defensive and may even view the challenge to excellence as a kind of putdown. While some shun the call to excellence in favor of coddling or mutual moaning, others take to it like a fish takes to water. It vivifies and refreshes, awakening a latent power, a sleeping giant within.

One of the great joys of my career consulting practice is to watch the power that believing in people (holding the expectation that they will be successful) has on them. For example, I worked with one woman who had been diagnosed with depression and agoraphobia. After years of therapy and psychiatric medications, she was at her wit's end. She had become so frightened of living that she was afraid even to leave her house. When she assured me that she was ready to follow my advice, I agreed to meet with her in her home.

Here was an attractive and wealthy young woman with no job, no children, and too much time on her hands. We set about at once brainstorming what kind of volunteer work she might be able to do immediately. In no time, she was working with handicapped children. One year later, she had established a nonprofit organization in another field. Instead of giving her pity or trying to solve her problem, I chose to ignore it. I assumed that she was fine and held up the expectation that she not only could but should be doing something for others. Soon she had new, more interesting, problems to think about; and in the process, she forgot her own. Today, this "depressed agoraphobic" travels the country inspiring others on behalf of a cause she deeply cares about.

I tell this story to emphasize that there is great power in believing in people *when they are open and ready to receive it.* Develop the discrimination to see who is and who isn't open to your help. Nothing you can say or do will help someone who doesn't want to be helped, and nothing is more frustrating for either party than trying to force the issue. If you find yourself struggling to change people who are not so inclined, recognize that you may be the one who needs a change. Develop the expectation that people are ready to receive your love and support, and find yourself some new friends. Remember, there are plenty of people out there who are ready to receive your encouragement and support with open arms. Struggling with those who don't want to change will only irritate them and leave you feeling frustrated and helpless. As in personal relationships, so too in work relationships: you deserve to work for or with people who appreciate your contributions.

Focusing Questions

- Of all the people you know, who is most consistently supportive of your goals and dreams? Who consistently holds high expectations of you and encourages you not to settle for less than your best?
- Is there anyone in your life who tends to be openly hostile or negative toward your dreams? If so, who? Do you have any "soft enemies"—people who appear supportive, but tend to encourage limited views of yourself? Who are they? How can you better protect yourself from these negative influences?
- List the names of people you would like to get to know better, people who could serve as role models or supportive friends.

JEALOUSY MAY OPEN THE DOOR TO GREATNESS

By carefully examining aspects of our character that are generally considered nasty or evil, we are often able to discover wonderful things about ourselves. Such is the case with jealousy. When we have fallen into settling for less and are unwilling to admit it or do anything about it, the jealousy we feel toward others may be an unconscious way of trying to tell ourselves what we really want.

There is some soul of goodness in things evil, would men observingly distill it out. —SHAKESPEARE

When using jealousy to help unlock your true desires, it does little good to focus on things such as, "I am jealous of so-and-so because he was born rich and gets all the breaks" or "I envy her because she is so beautiful and gets the attention I crave." Neither is it useful to envy others for their talents. We don't envy dogs because their hearing and sense of smell are better than ours, fish for being better swimmers, or birds because they fly. The bird who wishes he could swim with the fishes will miss the joys of finding his own wings.

Yet it may be useful to consider the envy we feel toward the accomplishments of others. For accomplishments are the result of effort, and we are always in control of the effort we make. Even for those with extraordinary talents, great accomplishment comes as the result of great effort. As Michelangelo said, "If people knew how hard I worked to get my mastery, it wouldn't seem so wonderful after all." To envy Michelangelo's talent will do us no good, but to envy (or admire) his hard work may inspire more of our own. As Johann Sebastian Bach put it, "I was made to work; if you are equally industrious, you will be equally successful."

Focusing Questions

- Whose accomplishments do you most envy? List the names of at least three people. (If you really feel as though you have no jealousy, then you can frame these questions in terms of the people whose accomplishments you most admire.)
- For each person, list at least three specific accomplishments that you most envy.
- Now review your answers and write down the top five accomplishments you are most jealous of.
- Finally, ask yourself how you can begin creating your own life so that you can accomplish similar things.

Excellence: A Matter of Dedication

Thousands of people have talent. I might as well congratulate you for having eyes in your head. The one and only thing that counts is: Do you have staying power? —NOEL COWARD

Why not just go from job to job? Why do you need a life's work anyway? The answer lies in the lessons which dedication alone can teach. Dedication reveals to you your inner strength, the depth of your love. Dedication provides a point of focus into which you can concentrate your energies, into which you can pour your heart. Dedication will also teach you commitment, and inevitably, it will teach you detachment. It will teach you when to pour on the extra effort and when to let go. Here, then, is another great key to the discovery of your life's work: Ask yourself, What am I willing to dedicate myself to?

We can be interested in many things, but only really dedicated to a few. Find a work that you are ready to dedicate yourself to, come what may. As Joseph Campbell put it, "Any life career that you choose in following your bliss should be chosen with [this] sense—that nobody can frighten you off from this thing. And no matter what happens, this is the validation of my life and action." When Mother Teresa was going through a period of self-questioning and doubt prior to finding her own life's work, she sought the advice of a wise man. She asked him how she would know if she had found her true calling in life. The advice he gave in reply is something we all do well to remember. As he told her, you will know you have found your work "if you are happy. . . . Profound joy of heart is like a magnet that indicates the path of life. One has to follow it even though one enters into a way full of difficulties."

This is what is meant by finding a life's work, by doing the work you love. It is not necessarily that it is always easy or even always pleasurable. On the contrary, true love has the element of sacrifice, a readiness to suffer for something greater than oneself. Yet, as Samuel Johnson put it, "He that labors in any great or laudable undertaking has his fatigues first supported by hope, and afterwards rewarded by joy."

Those who have found real success, whatever field they might work in, will tell you that the better part of success is persistence, sticking with it, refusing to give up. As Longfellow said, "Perseverance is a great element of success. If you only knock long enough and loud enough at the gate, you are sure to wake somebody up." So it is with finding the work you love. Keep on knocking until you wake yourself up to what you were born to do. The important thing is to stick with it. As Albert Schweitzer said, "Do not lose heart even if you must wait a bit before finding the right thing. Be prepared for disappointment, also! But do not abandon the quest."

Epilogue

From the Ideal to the Real Deal

Love makes one fit for any work. —GEORGE HERBERT

Once you have found the work you love, the next step is to make a career of it. Joseph Campbell gave a simple formula for doing the work you love: "First you must find your own trajectory and then comes the social coordination." Your "trajectory" is the *creative passion* of your life—the energy, motivation, and direction that comes from within. It is your calling, the work you love. Making the "social coordination" is the *creative challenge* of your life—the process through which you give your inner creative passion form and substance in the life of society.

In this book, we have outlined a number of things you can do to find your own trajectory, the work you love. This is, without a doubt, the single most important step to *doing* the work you love. For unless you start out on the right road, you haven't a chance of reaching your destination. To put it another way, you don't want to spend your life climbing the ladder of success only to discover that it was leaning against the wrong wall. Still, finding the work you love is only the first step. Once you are clear on what your work is, you will want to begin developing a strategy for shaping it into a viable career.

In any creative process, there is always a tension between the creative inspiration and the ability to give it shape and form within the limits of existing structures. Often people have wonderful visions of things they would like to do, yet because they are either unwilling or unable to create the necessary structures or to effectively interface with existing structures, they are unable to convert these dreams into realities. The basic structural limits you will encounter on the road to creating the work you love are the dynamics of the prevailing social organization and the limits of time.

Making the Social Coordination

Societal Structure: Along with family, work is the glue that holds society together. In turn, the structure of society shapes and limits the way we work. Our modern commercial culture is organized in terms of the marketplace, in other words, in terms of the money economy. Unlike the people of any other society in human history, we cannot live without money. This means that money and marketing become critical issues that must be addressed. It means that when we think about doing the work we love, we must think about how we will market that work. (We will have more to say about marketing yourself below.)

Career Structure: Every career field has a structure, a certain way the game is played. There are conventional ways of doing things in business, science, publishing, film-making, and in virtually any other field we may want to work in. Select a career field that allows you to be yourself and do the work you love. Choose a career through which you can fulfill your purpose and express your talents, one that *feels* right to you and where winning at the game will mean something to you.

Organizational Structure: The way work is organized also imposes structural limits on the way we work. The organization of work, which in the industrial period had grown highly centralized and bureaucratic, is currently undergoing a profound transformation. It is becoming in many ways less centralized, with large organizations employing fewer people, and less hierarchical, with individual workers being encouraged, and in many cases required, to take greater responsibility for the success of the organizations that employ them. The number of self-employed people who have opened up shop or started working freelance or in home-based businesses has risen steadily in recent years. On the other hand, large organizations are gaining dominance in service and retail sectors that were once the exclusive domain of small-time entrepreneurs. Any or all of these trends may have relevance for the way you work. You will need to consider what type and size of organization you want to work for, or alternatively, to create.

The individual companies or organizations that you may want to work for have their own structural limits, with a variety of rules and regulations that you must deal with in some way. It pays to investigate organizations you are considering working for and to identify those whose values and objectives coincide with your own. Choose organizations whose success you can in good conscience take responsibility for and ones that will give you the creative freedom to do so.

Legal Structure: Laws established by governments and the regulations of numerous government agencies also impose structural limits on the way we work. These may include legally mandated educational requirements, licensing, or certification requirements. If we want to go into business for ourselves or create nonprofit organizations, governmental rules and regulations become much more complicated and complex. All of these are elements of making the social coordination.

Doing It in Time

While social organization imposes structural limits on the way we work, the most basic of all limiting structures is time. There are only so many years in a life, weeks in a year, minutes in a day. The fact that we have a limited amount of time means we must learn to manage it well. This begins with making value choices, establishing priorities and goals. We maximize the time we have each day when we use it from the perspective of a long-range vision of what we want to accomplish in our lives. While you don't want to become a slave to schedule, it certainly helps to develop a plan for making the transition from the work you are doing now to the work you would truly love to do. That plan should include goals with definite target dates for accomplishing intermediate steps on the road to your new work.

The Work You Love: The Play of a Lifetime

Think of the process of creating the work you love in terms of launching a new play. Let's say you have written a terrific script. You want to turn this script, this set of ideas, into an action—to create an event in the world of society that others can experience. In order to perform your play, you will require a theater, a setting. Moreover, you will need a producer and director, actors, lighting technicians, set designers, stagehands, ticket takers, ushers, and more. All of this comprises a kind of structural platform necessary to perform the play. You also must attract an audience. You'll want to let people know about your offering and give them reasons why they ought to attend.

In this analogy, the script represents your vision of yourself doing the work you love. Before you will be ready to do that work, you must either gain the confidence and support of an existing theater company (employer) or create your own. In one way or another, you must create a platform or stage from which to do your work, and an audience for it. Moreover, you may need to learn new knowledge and gain additional skills before you will be ready to begin playing your new career role or in order to continue to excel in it. Establishing or acquiring a platform, creating an audience, and improving your skill repertoire may not seem to be as much fun or as exciting as doing the work you love itself. Still, it is important to accept these as necessary elements in realizing your dreams. In fact, without them, doing the work you love may well remain only a dream.

We address each of these areas below. In creating your platform and selecting your career role, be imaginative and resourceful in assessing your career options. In attracting an audience for your work, it helps to be aggressive in the way that you market yourself. In developing your skill repertoire, be open and flexible to a process of lifelong learning.

Choose Your Role: Find a Career You Can Live With

The career you choose in many ways limits and prescribes the role you play in society. When you meet someone for the first time and they ask what you do, they are attempting to discover the social status of the role you play. Most likely, they are not terribly interested in what you actually *do*. They want to determine how to relate to you, based on the role you play.

While society is primarily interested in your role, in what you "are," it is important (if you are to do the work you love) that you be more interested in what you *do*. Make your purpose primary and your career role secondary and you will stay on target. For example, to say, "I want to be a lawyer" tells us very little about what you want to do or accomplish—about what your purpose is. But if you say, "I want to protect the environment" or "I want to protect people from injustice," and determine that the best way for you to accomplish your purpose is to assume the role of a lawyer, you will be clear on what you are working for.

Again, the analogy of a play helps us to separate the

essential from the peripheral. We can learn from the play-bill the role a person plays. We go to see the play to discover what he actually does and, more importantly, why he does it. In the play of life, motivation counts; it reveals the essence of character.

When you concentrate on what you want to do rather than on what you want to be, it is easier to see how you can transfer knowledge and skill gained in one field into another. If you think you *are* an X and you now want to work as a Y, you may think there is nothing in what an X does that in any way applies to what a Y does. Yet if you do not indentify *yourself* with your current role, and step back a bit, you will immediately recognize a whole range of transferable skills. In all likelihood, you have already learned a great deal that you can apply to your new career. Take the time to make a complete inventory of your existing skills and consider how you can apply these in doing the work you love.

INVESTIGATE POTENTIAL CAREER OPTIONS

Since in choosing a career role you are delineating the structural parameters of your work life, it is imperative that you do adequate research before you commit yourself. One of the major reasons people find themselves in unhappy work situations is that they failed to adequately research the field before they became involved in it. This is a mistake we don't want to repeat. Retraining for a new career can be an expensive and time-consuming proposition. It is therefore one that should never be undertaken without adequate research to ensure that you will be happy doing the work you are training for.

The celebrated actor Robert de Niro has been described as "working like a detective" while preparing for a new acting role. He wants to gain as much information on, and firsthand experience of, the role as possible, before he attempts to portray it. In the same way, do your detective work before you commit yourself to a new career role. Make sure you understand exactly what is involved. Go to the library and do research; and by all means, conduct informational interviews, that is, talk to a number of people who work in the career fields you are considering.

BE RESOURCEFUL IN PROVING YOUR QUALIFICATIONS

There is more than one way to skin a cat. Be creative and resourceful when it comes to demonstrating your qualifications or establishing credibility in your new career field. It may not be necessary, or even advisable, to return to school for formal retraining. Buckminster Fuller wanted to work as a scientist and engineer. Yet since he didn't have a college degree, he couldn't get published in the scientific journals. Instead of laboring in an academic environment he found tedious, Fuller devised an alternative strategy for creating credibility. He filed a number of patents for inventions and processes which he had developed. His motive was not financial reward (securing these patents cost him far more money than they ever made him) but professional respect. Documenting the original and exciting work he was doing helped him to be taken seriously by other scientists. Fuller went on to achieve worldwide fame as a "modern genius." You too may discover alternate routes to establishing your qualifications or enhancing your credibility.

Even where educational credentials are legally or otherwise mandated, it is often possible to acquire these without returning to school on a full-time basis. Today, a number of reputable universities and colleges offer degree credit for life experience, evening and weekend classes, as well as correspondence courses.

Begin doing the work you love as soon as possible, even if you don't get paid for it, or if you can only work at it part-time. Albert Einstein was unable to secure a job as a physics professor. (Apparently, no one thought he was sufficiently qualified.) He could have said to himself, "Well, I just don't have what it takes to work in physics. I should give up on it and settle for something else." Instead, he wrote the two most significant papers of his remarkable career while employed as a patent clerk. After their publication, there was not a major university in the world that would not have been delighted to have him on their staff.

The Wright brothers were not professional scientists but the owners of a small bicycle shop who had a passion for exploring the possibilities of manned flight. Time and again, avocations or hobbies turn out to be an individual's true calling. Start the business you are dreaming of out of your home or garage (Apple Computers began this way), even if you can only work at it during evenings and weekends. Begin doing volunteer work or take an internship in the field you want to work in. There is something about getting started in the work you love that attracts opportunities and opens doors.

Claim and affirm the work you love, even if it doesn't pay the bills. If you want to work as an artist and you are making your living as a waiter, don't think of yourself as a waiter who hopes one day to become an artist. That puts the work you love somewhere off in the distant future. Rather, think of yourself as an artist, temporarily supporting yourself by waiting tables—*and* paint, draw, or sculpt as much as you can. It is possible to earn a living wage as a waiter working twenty-five hours a week (at some of the better restaurants in the major cities). That leaves plenty of time to devote to training or developing your craft in the off hours. Or simplify your lifestyle and reduce the number of hours you work at your current job. Even without a change in lifestyle, most people can find ten to twelve hours a week to devote to retraining, developing their craft, or working part-time in their new career—if they *really* want to.

Create an Audience: Aggressively Market Yourself

No matter how good the play, how beautiful the theater, or how great the company, without an audience, the show closes. Creating and maintaining an audience for your work is essential to having a long career of great performances. Your audience is not necessarily the people whom you serve in your work. Your audience is made up of the people who *pay* to see you perform. Whether the audience you must create is an employer, a client base for your services, a steady stream of customers for your products, or contributors to your nonprofit foundation—you can bet that sooner or later you will find yourself in competition. Others will be seeking the attention and support of your potential audience.

ACCEPT MARKETING AS A FACT OF LIFE

The Chinese have a saying: "The marketplace is a battlefield." If indeed this is so, then it pays to approach it with the attitude of a warrior. Go to the marketing battlefield like a true warrior, courageous, skillful, full of integrity, and ready to fight for what you believe in. Of course, the marketing battle really begins in your own heart. It is there that you must slay the dragons of doubt and vanquish the notion of settling for less than your best. It is there that you must be convinced that there is a place for you in this world, a way for you to express yourself through the work you love. If you win this battle, you won't fear rejection or competition. If you lose it, you'll never know what you might have accomplished.

Another aspect of being a warrior is the capacity to see things as they really are and to develop effective strategies for dealing with them. Though we may wish it otherwise, a good look at the commercial culture we live in forces us to accept the need to market ourselves and our work. After all, unless you achieve a certain measure of success in the marketplace, you'll have to give up on doing the work you love and settle for something less. Fight for what you want. Get active and aggressive in pursuing it. Don't squander your aggressive energy in frustration, resentment, hostility, or self-sabotage; channel it into creating the life you want by making a place in the market for the work you love.

IMPROVE YOUR MARKETING SKILLS

It takes more than courage to succeed in the marketing battle. It takes skill. No matter what kind of work you intend to do, you increase your chances of success by improving your marketing skills. Today, in a very real sense, everyone is self-employed and must know how to attract and communicate with an audience, be it an audience of one or of thousands. Almost anyone could benefit from training in sales or public speaking. Marketing is, after all, simply the ability to effectively communciate a message.

If doing the work you love requires securing employment within existing organizations, set about improving your job-hunting skills. Determine to make mastery of the job-hunting process a vital and reliable component of your skill repertoire. Keep in mind the fact that more than eighty percent of all jobs are never advertised. Don't expect the job you want to come to you. Know how to go out and get it, and determine that you will. There is nothing more absurd than remaining in a job you don't like simply because you feel intimidated by the prospect of looking for another. Knowledge and skill breed confidence, and confidence is critical to success in the marketplace.

The basic job-hunting skills you will want to develop are targeting potential employers, securing interviews, and excelling at them. These are relatively simple skills that can be easily acquired by virtually anyone, with minimal time and expense. Check with community or vocational colleges and adult education or university extension programs in your area. If you are currently unemployed, there may be federally funded programs in your area.

If the work you love requires working freelance or establishing your own business, plan to develop your entrepreneurial skills. Begin taking classes and seminars and reading on subjects such as small business start-up, finance and accounting, marketing, sales, advertising, publicity, and so on. If the best platform for the work you love is a nonprofit organization, in addition to developing many of the entrepreneurial skills listed above, you'll want to develop fundraising and grant proposal writing skills. The point is, whatever platform you choose, make a long-term commitment to developing your marketing skills.

PERSEVERANCE FURTHERS

The critical test of the warrior's character is perseverance, the capacity to endure. Ultimate victory cannot be denied anyone who simply refuses to give up. Learn to let rejection and disappointment roll off your back. And keep coming. You never know if the next interview, the next book or grant proposal, the next audition or recital will be the one that launches your new career. Hang in there and keep coming. As Syrus said, "Do not turn back when you are just at the goal." Often the person who succeeds is simply the one who is still willing to try after everyone else has given up.

Expand Your Repertoire:
Commit to Lifelong Learning

Creating the work we love requires that we know what we want to do, that we choose a career field that allows us to do it, that we aggressively put ourselves and our work out there in the marketplace, and that we continue to grow, both in terms of competency in our craft and as human beings.

Like knowing how to market yourself, lifelong learning is a necessity in today's work environment. As John Naisbitt, author of *Megatrends*, has written: "In the new information society, where change is the only constant, we can no longer expect to get an education and be done with it. There is no one education or skill that lasts a lifetime now. Like it or not, the information society has turned us all into lifelong learners."

More important than what you have already learned is that you know *how to learn,* that you can quickly acquire and integrate new knowledge and skills. In many fields today, knowledge becomes obsolete in a matter of a few years; in some, in a matter of months. Moreover, most of the new jobs today are being created by small business. Small organizations prefer flexible people who are "quick studies" over those who are highly specialized in a single area of expertise. Of course, for those planning on starting their own organizations, everything we have said about the value of being versatile and a quick learner goes double.

Beyond being an economic necessity, lifelong learning is a basic requirement of a happy and healthy life. When we stop learning, we stop growing, and in a way, stop living. Determine to continue learning and growing, not only in terms of your skill and knowledge, but in terms of your character and wisdom. Often we learn the most from failure and disappointment. When things don't go our way or when we must confront untoward changes beyond our control, we find out what we are really made of and discover what is really important in life.

MAKE FRIENDS WITH CHANGE

Like it or not, change is a fact of life. Change is growth, new things being born, and change is death, old things dying away. The biggest mistake is to assume that things will remain as they are. To be happy and successful, then, we must learn to embrace and not resist change. We must learn to change on purpose, to seek deliberately and consciously to grow in competency and character. Moreover, we must learn to embrace changes beyond our control and to respond to them in a constructive and creative manner.

When it comes to changing on purpose, there are two basic categories of change to consider: inner changes and outer changes. Inner changes include changes in our self-esteem, attitudes, and expectations, in the ways we approach and respond to the events of our lives. Outer changes may include changes in career field, skill level or work habits, associates, geographic location, or immediate work environment. Make a list of the inner and outer changes that will facilitate you doing the work you love.

Doing the Work You Love: An Expanding Focus

The process of creating the work you love requires the balanced use of both right and left brain capacities. In other words, it requires the ability to both expand and contract (or focus) your awareness. While seeking to discover the work you love, it helps to expand your awareness into the universe of all possibilities. You don't want to be limited to preconceived ideas of what you should do or confined to what you have done before. Having opened to all possibilities, you then focus again by making a definite decision and claiming the work you love as your own. You decide what you are working for.

You expand your awareness again by considering and investigating various career roles—all the ways you could go about doing that work. You focus again by selecting a specific career path and developing a plan for marketing yourself in that career. You expand again as you grow in competency, gaining additional knowledge and skill, and so on. This is the process: expanding and then focusing your awareness, breathing in new possibilities and integrating them into everyday life.

The trick is to know when to open up and expand and when to concentrate and focus. If we are open to creative inspirations but unable to focus by making choices and developing strategies for their implementation, we risk spending our lives in a dream world. On the other hand, if our focus is too narrow, we are liable to get into a rut of habit and routine. Opening to new inspirations, strategies, and knowledge refreshes and renews.

Doing the work you love, then, requires that you be equally comfortable with the imaginative and the practical. It requires the ability to dream big dreams and the ability to confront and master all the little details that go into making dreams come true. Best of luck to you in following your dreams. May you have a lifetime of joy and adventure doing the work you love!

A Final Note

The process of finding and doing the work you love is addressed in considerably more detail in *Zen and the Art of Making a Living: A Practical Guide to Creative Career Design* by the author of the present work. For more on the process of finding the work you love, refer to the section entitled "The Quest for Life's Work" and complete the accompanying exercises. The remainder of the book is dedicated to assisting you in designing a program for turning the work you love into a viable career. In addition to information on developing a strategy for making the transition into the work you love, this book provides specific information on assessing your skills, landing the right job, starting your own business, working freelance, starting your own non-profit organization, and much more. At over six hundred pages, this is a reference you can refer to again and again.

For career information, resources, links, and more, visit
The Center for Creative Empowerment at:
www.empoweryou.com

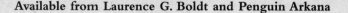